DESIGN FOR YOU

DESIGN FOR YOU

FIRST EDITION

ETHEL JANE BEITLER
Texas Technological College

BILL LOCKHART
Texas Technological College

JOHN WILEY & SONS, INC., NEW YORK · LONDON

DEDICATED TO LETTA

TO START WITH

DESIGN FOR YOU was chosen as our title because it emphasizes the various ways in which we may study, see, produce, or appreciate organizations of lines, shapes, spaces, colors, and textures as they are created for use in our everyday lives. The designs may represent the plan of a building, a drawing of a bowl to be turned on a lathe, a sketch of a design to be scratched in clay and sand for a wallpiece, or the design for a piece of jewelry, a dress, a bag, a mural, or a piece of sculpture. There is no limit.

The ideas throughout this book are the outgrowth of work with students in classes in Freshman Design. Our contacts have been mainly with students who have come to college with little or no previous art training. They may not understand the goals of the artist and his philosophy or the techniques he uses. We do feel, however, that most individuals have an appreciation for beauty and a sense of order. It is a source of gratification for students to realize that they are also capable of creating their own designs.

It is our hope that the information in these chapters will be of value to anyone interested in developing an appreciation of art. We hope that teachers will find this book helpful in developing in their students a working knowledge of basic factors in the organization and evaluation of designs of their own and those of the past. We also hope that the book will be a definite aid to those interested in the expression of originality.

Heretofore, some instructors have made many attempts to introduce the art student to the meaning of design by concentrating on the "principles of design." Others have cast aside all this disciplined study and have used an experimental approach, hoping that the student would absorb a working knowledge of how to create and evaluate his designs by working with materials in a more or less trial-and-error method. Although few have enough imagination or attain great technical ability to become artists of note, we feel nevertheless that everyone can attain some appreciation that encompasses both intellectual understanding and emotional response to his own designs as well as to those created by ones more talented than he. We also feel that a certain amount of rational or disciplined study as suggested in these chapters will help the student to achieve a sensitivity to ways of applying the principles of design with a certain amount of skill.

In our civilization it is necessary for us to be able to read and write even if we are not authors. Similarly it should be necessary for the student of art to acquire a vocabulary of terms pertaining to his creative experiences that he can understand and use. This knowledge should in no way hinder his creative thinking. On the contrary, it should stimulate it and enable him to have more logical reasons for his original experiments.

Thus we have tried in the following chapters to:

(1) combine this basic knowledge of art terms both in vocabulary and in background for evaluation, and

(2) give suggestions for creative experiences, and

(3) help the student appreciate the important place that art occupies in our everyday lives.

The discussions of art terms and the experiments are concentrated on the visual arts only. The suggested experiments are planned to go from the more simple two-dimensional to the more complex three-dimensional ones.

The information concerning the principles of design has been grouped in one chapter, whereas each element of design is given a separate chapter. Although this arrangement may imply that we feel the elements are more important, this is not our purpose. We feel, however, that the approach to creative design can be motivated more successfully by concentrating on the elements. The principles become, then, important guideposts for evaluating their organization.

No statement or exercise should be interpreted as a formula or pattern to be followed in toto. The teacher or student may find the exercises at the ends of each chapter a way of leading him into free experimentation so that he becomes more conscious of his own resources. We hope that each will use his own imagination to adapt these exercises to his particular needs, tools, materials, and techniques.

We wish to thank Design Today, Inc. for their generosity in allowing us to photograph many contemporary items in their shop.

Our special thanks go to our co-workers and students in the Department of Applied Arts for their many helpful suggestions and for their constant loyal support in this work. We hope they may find this book "the" text for which they have been searching!

ETHEL JANE BEITLER

BILL LOCKHART

May, 1961

CONTENTS

LIST OF ILLUSTRATIONS

chapter 3 **WHAT'S YOUR LINE?**

chapter 4   **THE SHAPE OF THINGS**

chapter 8   **DESIGNING WITH THE ABC'S**

chapter 9   **DESIGN SPEAKS OUT**

1

DESIGN FOR OUR AGE

Over the generations the taste of the designer has constantly altered. Many factors that may cause these changes are (1) the designer's educational background; (2) the available materials, tools, machines, and other equipment that might be utilized by the designer; (3) the purpose for which he plans his design; and (4) his ability to cope with the changes in civilization over a period of time. All of these, and many more, are sufficient causes for the constant succession of designs. The variations become obvious when we compare the Wright brothers' first airplane to present-day jet airliners. Each improvement in air power necessitated alterations in basic design. The autogyro, which was flown in the 1930's, was the first attempt to develop an airplane that was capable of vertical flight. The autogyro was a conventional type of airplane, with minor modification, and with a large rotary blade mounted on top of the plane. This plane was flown with some success, but made little contribution to air transportation. During the early 1940's, however, the helicopter made a major contribution to air transportation. Probably the difference in the success of these two similar aircraft was in the design, for the helicopter was not dependent upon modification of the original airplane. The designers of the helicopter had to modify their concept of what an aircraft should look like. There is no progress without change, but change is not necessarily progress. It is highly desirable that these changes be beneficial to mankind. Our main problem is to be able to discriminate between that which should be discarded and that which should be kept, built upon, and improved.

Design, broadly interpreted, refers to:

1. A particular design for a special object of art.
2. Selection and arrangement of those selections for a particular purpose.
   a. That purpose may be a utilitarian one, such as planning the height of a lamp and the width of the shade to give a wide enough spread of light for ease in reading.
   b. The purpose may be an esthetic one, such as planning the height of a lamp and the width of the shade to give a sense of pleasing proportions in relation to the table on which the lamp is placed and the chair beside it.

A design may suit a utilitarian purpose but be sadly lacking in qualities that might give it beauty, or vice versa. The spout of a coffee pot may be excellent for pouring but difficult to clean. The lines of the coffee pot may give it a quality of stateliness and grace, yet it may be very inconvenient because the top keeps falling off when it is tilted for pouring.

The purpose of this book is not to set up rules of organization for the elements of design, but rather to help the student of design to develop a philosophy or creative approach to design—"a way of life." This awareness should enable him to appreciate the works of other artists in his own and earlier periods. This book should give the student the ability to apply simple basic principles so that his own designs will show that character and individuality which represent his own personality and way of working to the best of his ability. A design student may look about until he finds an interesting scrap of wood which suggests to him the shape of a giraffe. He may go on to do a bit of carving and shaping to strengthen that idea and finish with a piece of wood sculpture depicting a giraffe. Another student may say, "I'm going to make a giraffe," and proceed to look for an appropriate piece of wood which could be used for that purpose. By either method, the end result would be the same. One starts with the material and lets it suggest to him what he can do with it. The other has a definite idea in mind before he selects the material and then chooses it and works with it accordingly. Lack of knowledge of the materials and proc-

Fig. 1-1. Present-day machine-made furniture makes no attempt to copy the designs of the past. Metal framework used with wood for drawers and shelves, cabinets with hard plastic tops, and adjustable arrangements harmonize with our contemporary scheme of living. (Comprehensive Storage System designed by George Nelson for the Herman Miller Furniture Company.)

Fig. 1-2. The FireHOOD represents a new concept of design for warmth and beauty in a contemporary home. (Courtesy of Condon-King Co., Inc.)

Fig. 1-3. A student design for a hooked rug could be used satisfactorily as an area rug or as a gay wall panel.

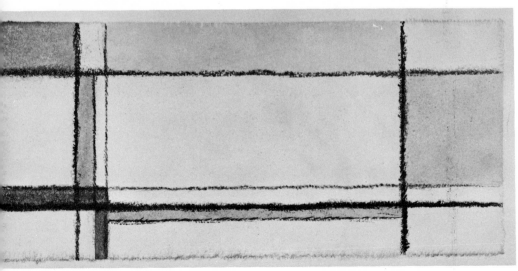

ess, however, may cause the student to attempt to force his material into a desired shape. This student would be unsuccessful with the second method and would do well either to use the first method or to experiment with his material sufficiently until he knows how to select his material and work with it to create the desired design. Before planning a design, a student should explore the possibilities of the materials available to him. As the designer becomes better acquainted with his materials and processes, his work will evidence more unity between the design and materials used.

This exploring of a material, even though it is one with which the student is familiar, may lead to many new and exciting discoveries of its personality and character. It becomes increasingly important for the designer to re-examine constantly processes and the materials which he uses. For example, most people think that they are familiar with paper, yet how many have examined the numerous ways in which paper is used in today's society? Everyone has folded paper, but few people have seen the delightful curves which may be folded in a piece of paper. Paper—one of the flimsier materials—may be folded and creased so that it gains the strength to stand by itself. In fact, not only may it stand, but two sheets of construction paper, weighing a fraction of an ounce, are capable of supporting fifteen or twenty pounds of weight. Thus, the student who sees new possibilities in the use of paper will be in a good position to apply new and exciting designs to paper. The same is true of all materials. Not only must we examine our materials, but we must also examine the ways and methods in which we each work best. As in the case of materials, each individual has his strengths and limitations. We should each work in a way best suited to our temperaments and individual abilities.

Design today, as always, is directed by the combination of tools and materials, methods of construction, and purpose or use of the design. The familiar statement that "form follows function" may not be as clear to some as the statement that "function should determine form and form should express function." But tradition hampers us in spite of our best intentions. For generations, we have associated the design of a table knife with that of a long, narrow blade. A designer is ridiculed when he insists that the blade can just as well be short and broad to give one the

5

Fig. 1-4. Students who in the past had worked with paper only in a flat form found it exciting to experiment with paper in a three-dimensional manner.

Fig. 1-5. Using a natural form for inspiration, a student may create an abstract form that has personality and intriguing details.

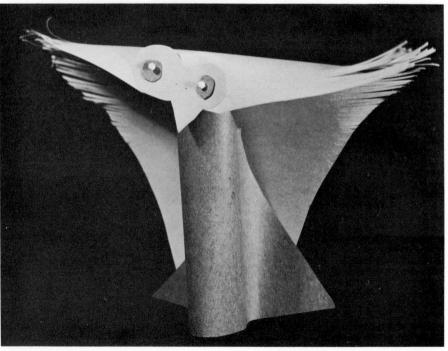

ample length for cutting purposes and the width necessary for spreading butter. We may have been accustomed to the long, thin tines on a table fork on which it is difficult to balance peas. Yet we are reluctant to accept a new design of a fork with short, broad tines and a curved bowl to keep the peas from falling off. The creator of this new knife and fork is only trying to design forms that are determined by the uses that are made of them in cutting, spreading, and transferring food from the plate to the mouth. When we say that "form expresses function," we sense a desire on our part to really use this knife to cut or to spread butter.

Our designs are what they are because of the materials used in them. Every material, whether it is wood, metal, glass, or plastic, has qualities which make it suitable for particular uses. When we emphasize that fact and do not let tradition interfere and tempt us to make a metal chair frame look like a wooden one, we shall have greater variety of designs which are more beautiful and practical.

In the furnishing of our homes, it seemed inevitable that our early machine-made furniture should try to imitate the work of the skilled cabinetmaker and carver. As machine production grew into mass production, the need to simplify operations and reduce costs produced two results. One was the elimination of the extra details, and the other was poor workmanship. Gradually there emerged the realization that wood itself is beautiful in its exposed, undecorated state. It is available in a great variety of forms and quantities. It lends itself to a multitude of techniques with which it can be turned into objects of beauty.

Then in the last century along came the designer who conceived the idea that furniture could be made of metal. Unfortunately, tradition stunted his imagination. Like his ancestors who had tried to imitate the skilled carvers in their machine-made designs, he imitated the designs in wood. The metal products were even painted and grained to simulate the exact appearance of wood. Fairly recently we have realized that we can design beautiful furniture which is frankly made of metal, undisguised, and in new forms suited to the natural material of metal rather than of wood. We know that such furniture can have sparkle, grace, charm, comfort, and durability. We know, also, that if we want the other virtues of warmth, richness, and traditional beauty we can turn to wood, proving that we can plan a design that best suits the material.

Fig. 1-6. The variation of the thickness and the contour of the vase lends a simple dignity to the shape. The lack of ornamentation also emphasizes the pleasing use of glass as a material. (Orefors crystal, courtesy Zacho, Inc.)

Fig. 1-7. The sculptural beauty of the hand-wrought sterling has a flowing quality of dignified beauty. Note the curved "spoonlike" quality of the forks. ("Tjorn" pattern designed by Jens H. Quistgaard for Dansk Designs, Inc., Great Neck, New York.)

Fig. 1-8. "Focus" pattern in stainless steel, chosen one of the 100 best designs of our time, utilizes the design of the short blade on the knife. (Designed by Folke Arstrom for Gense, Import, Ltd.)

We can go further in our discussion of the knife and fork and compare the early designs in stainless steel tableware with traditional ones in silver. The idea was prevalent in the minds of housewives that silver was the only beautiful material for flatware. Therefore, when stainless steel designers attempted to get their ideas accepted, they imitated the earlier patterns in silver, making it look cheap and penny-saving. When designers and consumers were willing to open their eyes to the beauty of stainless steel as a material, the designers could then begin to create the simple, unadorned, and sculptured forms that the housewife had to admit she had admired all along but was afraid to select in silver because it was easily scratched and marred.

It is no less important for those of us who are consumers to have a knowledge of art quality than it is for us who are merchants with the responsibility of stocking our shelves with items for others to buy. The merchant is naturally interested in the money value of an object, but in most cases that object will have greater sale value if it is well designed.

On the other side of the picture, it is evident that the ability to recognize good art quality is not always sufficient. Many times there are definite limitations to the expression of good taste.

1. The likes and dislikes of people who are going to use the items.
2. The availability of items limited because of certain economic or political upheavals or shortage of materials.
3. The number or kind of items one has on hand.
4. The prevailing fashions.

All the above might cause us to alter our choices, regardless of our store of knowledge of basic principles of design. If we can learn to make wise choices, considering both utility and beauty, and learn to live with our selections and be just plain happier, then art has found a definite place in our daily lives.

What is the role of the student in developing skills and understanding of design? No text or course by itself can guarantee that a student will develop the knowledge and understanding of design. There must be a willingness and an interest. He must study, see, feel, and evaluate his reactions. The student must explore and experiment. To gain a knowl-

Fig. 1-9. Architects are introducing new materials and new lines into our church designs. Here the sweeping curves of the vaulted roof eliminate entirely the side walls of stained glass windows. (First Presbyterian Church, Levelland, Texas. Architects and Engineers, A.I.A., Schmidt and Stuart.)

edge of design, he must be willing to examine his prejudices and be flexible. No written material will explain design unless the student makes an effort to examine what is presented. Many points may seem strange and even shocking. What if traditional church architecture as built today is criticized as being poor taste? Are you as a student willing to examine this statement? Could there be truth in such shocking words? Many times your emotional attachments may make you intolerant. Deep personal involvement with religion and warm feelings for the place of worship make it hard to accept criticism of a place of worship. If you tell one that his church is poorly designed, his first reaction is apt to be negative. He may feel that you are criticizing his church, his religion, and even himself. To become a real student of design, one must be willing to examine his surroundings critically, even though many of these objects may be important for sentimental reasons. One must attempt to be as objective as possible, although it is doubtful that any person can become completely objective. One must recognize that our emotional make-up will have much to do with the light in which we view design.

Each design we make is a definite act. It may be one of imitation or one which represents creative thinking. Whether we are *designing* or creating a *design,* we assemble *lines, shapes* or forms, *textures,* and *colors* in a *space.* These, then, are referred to as the *elements of design.* They are the tools and materials with which everyone makes a design. Over the past century or more our attitude toward "design" has gradually changed. Formerly it was more frequently thought of in relation to an applied decoration or pattern, such as wallpaper or printed fabric. Today we refer more to the *act of designing* which encompasses all our acts of selection and arrangement. Those may include the problem of selecting lines and colors for a design on the drawing board, or selecting lines and colors for the furnishings of a room. Thus design is a problem for everyone, not just for students with so-called artistic ability. Consequently, we need a thorough background in an appreciation of the *elements of design,* how to create with them, and evaluate their arrangement according to the *principles of balance, proportion, emphasis,* and *rhythm.* In the following chapters we shall strive to provide that background.

2

GUIDEPOSTS FOR ORGANIZATION

Our taste is reflected in the things we select. Our training, understanding, and experiences are responsible for molding our tastes. If we are flexible in our attitudes and have acquired a treasure house of knowledge that should aid us in making our selections, then we are never forced to make a poor choice through lack of knowledge. We must learn to make our training and experiences work for us so we can learn to get the most out of our facilities. It is said that there are none so blind as those who will not see. It is not expected that everyone with the same training and experience will make the same selections. There are always personal reasons for likes and dislikes which may alter one's choices, but the fact remains that the person who will not make use of his training to aid him in making wiser choices and who chooses items only because he likes them, with no logical reasons to explain his selections, may soon find himself set in his ways and inclined to be narrow minded in his tastes.

All our acts of selection and arrangement are decisions in design. Whether it is in the painting of a picture, the carving of a piece of wood sculpture, the planting of a garden, or in the selection and arrangement of furnishings for a room, we are making a design decision. This decision involves our likes and dislikes, our human needs, and the application of the guideposts for organization or the *principles of design:* balance, proportion, emphasis, and rhythm.

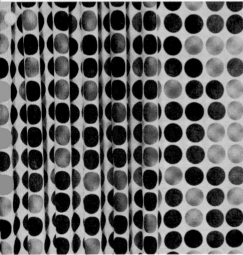

(upper left)
Fig. 2-1. Regular repeats which satisfy because of the roughness of the stone that supplies the variety. (Yucatan Stone from Murals, Inc.)

(upper right)
Fig. 2-2. Irregularity of sizes of the same shape provide variety with unity. (Yucatan Stone from Murals, Inc.)

(lower left)
Fig. 2-3. Regular repeats of circles which satisfy because of the irregular variation of values of dark and light. ("Circles," designed by Alexander Girard for Herman Miller Furniture Company.)

(lower right)
Fig. 2-4. Irregularity of sizes of the same shape again provides variety with unity. ("One-Way," designed by Alexander Girard for the Herman Miller Furniture Company.)

All of us work (1) *in a variety of ways* when we create designs. No two people will approach a problem in exactly the same manner. All of us have (2) *different needs* that will alter our choices. Those needs may be economic, physical, psychological, or emotional. (3) The *materials* that are available at the time we are planning the design will most assuredly influence our choices. At no time in history has the designer had such a profusion of materials with which to work as he has today. This fact alone might actually make the designer's task more difficult because of the vast store of knowledge he needs concerning the possibilities and limitations of all these materials. (4) The *locality* where the design is created and used will be evident in its organization. This is especially obvious in home architecture; warmer climates influence the architectural design. (5) The *tools and processes* used in the development of the design will alter an individual's approach to the problem. When we group all these factors with the application of principles of design and allow for changes resulting from our many likes and dislikes, it is no wonder that there is no end to our changing designs.

All the above factors show a need for basic aims of organization which can be applied in any area of design. First, we must strive for a *sense of order*—of unity—of oneness. This order can be of a regimental type—a planned example of regularity which still satisfies us because of the pleasing way in which the proportions of the various parts of the repeat have been organized. For an all-over pattern for wallpaper, gift-wrapping papers, printed fabric design, or floor covering one might find it to his advantage to plan a regimental type of pattern. This order can be of a nonregimental type. It should be spontaneous, free, a planned form of irregularity that tickles the palette, intrigues the eye, amuses us, satisfies us, or just plain delights us with a feeling of rightness. But whether we plan a regular or an irregular pattern to achieve order, we need to know how to apply the principles of design—proportion, balance, emphasis, and rhythm—guides in using the plastic elements of lines, shapes, colors, textures, and space which compose our design. (For examples of regular and irregular repeats, see photographs in Figs. 2-1, 2, 3, and 4.)

Order implies a feeling of sameness or unity, but we need to go further than just a trite application of principles of design and arrive at a *sense of beauty* achieved through a knowledge of when to vary that sameness. To

Fig. 2-5. Glassware assumes a quality of formality or informality because of its length of stem or weight. "Tango" pattern in Royal Leerdam is more informal because of the short stems on the iced tea and sherbet. This set was awarded the hallmark of "Good Design" of the New York Museum of Modern Art. Designed by A. D. Copier. (Photograph courtesy of A. J. Van Dugteren and Sons, Inc.)

(lower left)
Fig. 2-6. "Patrician" pattern in Lobmeyr crystal is delicate, fragile in appearance, and very formal in character because of its tall, thin stem. (Executed by J. and L. Lobmeyr, Vienna, Austria. Designed by Professor Joseph Hoffman of the Vienna Academy of Applied Arts, 1918.)

(lower right)
Fig. 2-7. "Princess" pattern in Danish crystal is heavy, because of its thick base, and presents a more informal air. (Photograph courtesy of Gematex, Inc.)

know when and where to introduce *variety* in unity necessitates constant observation, study, experimentation, and practice to arrive at the point where we can say that we can create a good design. (See Figs. 2-1, 2, 3, and 4.)

Over and above all this, there must be the *creative factor* which sets one design apart from another and gives it life and meaning. This creative element is difficult to analyze and logically explain. It is either present or absent. It may be favored or disfavored by circumstances. Walter Dorwin Teague in *Design This Day* states of the contemporary designer:

> There is no school where he can acquire even a trace of talent. . . . But if he has a spark in him, the world today is full of many winds that will make it blaze. . . . There is a world around us to be rebuilt and the man who does not take fire at the prospect of a share in the job had better realize at once that he has no creative gift and take employment under someone who has: then at least he will be in the fight and share its excitement.

P R O P O R T I O N

Proportion is the principle of design that involves a pleasing relationship between all parts of the design in relation to each other and to the whole.

1. This principle may include the planning of the *basic shapes* within a design. Shall we use a rectangle instead of a square? Shall we use a parallelogram or a free-form? Shall we use a reverse curve or a semicircle? Besides the esthetic approach, do we need to consider physical contact, such as the shape of a handle to fit the hand or the contour of a chair to fit the body?

2. It may involve the *scale* of the forms within the design. Shall we use large forms, small ones, medium ones, or a combination of these?

3. How shall we *divide the space* for the over-all design and each of its parts and/or group the various sizes together? How can we achieve beautiful space relationships where variety of shape, size, and the general unity of idea are to be expressed?

4. How can we *create satisfying optical illusions* that will give the impression of beautiful proportions when it is not possible or feasible to change the basic design?

17

A

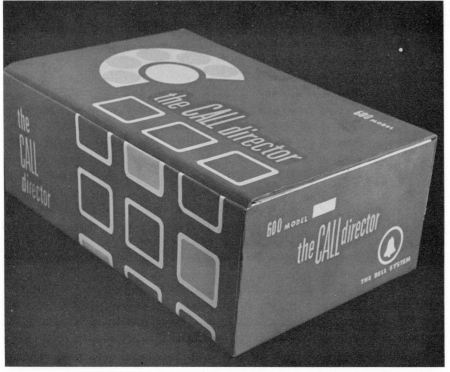

B

Fig. 2-8A and B. Although the proportions were determined by the suggested contents of the package, the decorative designs show a sensitive relationship to the structural form. (Class project designed by Jerry Stevens, student in Architecture and Allied Arts Department, Texas Technological College.)

PLANNING THE BASIC SHAPE

In Chapter 4 on shape and form there is a more extensive discussion of these elements from the standpoint of their selection and use in a design. At this point, we are mainly interested in the way in which the element of shape is involved with the principle of proportion. With each of the principles of design there are no rigid laws that can or should be applied in the development of a design. There are suggestions, however, which might aid the student or amateur artist in acquiring a feeling for good design.

In creating beautiful proportions, one suggestion might be inspired from the statement of John Dewey: "There is no excellent beauty that hath not some strangeness in the proportion." This does not mean, of course, that every object which is unusual in form, fantastic, exotic, or grotesque is beautiful in proportion. "Strangeness" in this sense would mean that one refrains from too much repetition and knows when to introduce just enough variety to add interest. That variety may be in the tumbler which is tapered at the bottom to keep the proportions of the sides from expressing too much sameness. It may also be tapered to make it more convenient to grasp in the hand or it may be larger at the top to make it easier to clean.

In general, shapes which are just as wide as they are tall may not be as pleasing as those which vary in their horizontal and vertical measurements. The purpose for which the design is to be used and the processes to be followed in the completion of the project may determine to a great extent the ways in which we may successfully apply the principle of proportion. The design of a cardboard carton to be used in marketing a product might need to have straight sides so that the cartons could be stacked next to each other and on top of one another. The height, width, and depth of the carton would need to be planned in proportions which would enclose most satisfactorily the product to be marketed, and which could be made most economically from available cardboard stock. This carton might possibly develop into one which was cubical in shape, having the same rather monotonous vertical and horizontal measurements. For a utilitarian object such as this, however, the proportions would more likely be planned to suit the purpose of the design, and the art quality or beauty would be

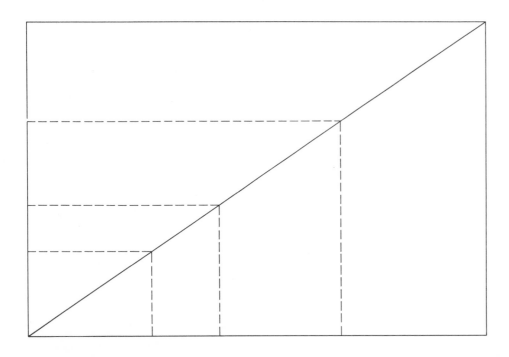

Fig. 2-9. Any square or rectangular shape may be reduced in scale and kept the same shape by dividing diagonally through the center and drawing lines parallel to the sides of the original shape.

(lower left)
Fig. 2-10. A small-scale drapery design harmonizes with the more delicate, curved-line furniture. ("Manhattan," designed by Alexander Girard for the Herman Miller Furniture Company.)

(lower right)
Fig. 2-11. A large-scale drapery design harmonizes with simple, straight-line furniture. ("Giant Rectangles," designed by Alexander Girard for the Herman Miller Furniture Company.)

expressed in the accuracy of workmanship and in the easy manipulation in the opening and closing of the carton.

On the other hand, if one were planning the proportions of a box to be used as a jewelry case, there would be no limitations such as the storage and marketing problems mentioned in the design of the cardboard carton. One could plan the jewelry case to be longer than deep, and the height shorter than the depth. The sides could be vertical or sloped, curved or straight; the edge could be sharp or rounded. The main problem would be (1) to plan a pleasing ratio between all measurements to avoid too much sameness or too much variety; (2) to plan a design which was not like every other jewelry box on the market, but which expressed a new quality in design which gave one a satisfied feeling of beauty; and (3) to plan it to meet the function of holding the specific pieces of jewelry for which it was designed.

SCALE

To be completely sensitive to beautiful proportions, one must be familiar with the underlying significance of scale. This is the relationship between sizes within an object and those of other objects used with it. Scale involves an understanding of the principle of ratios. We may observe that one rectangle is two inches wide and three inches long; it is the ratio of 2:3. Another rectangle is four inches wide and six inches long. It also is the ratio of 2:3; therefore, it is the same proportion as the first rectangle, but it is twice as large in scale. The graphic artist is well aware of this principle when he plans art work for reproduction purposes. He knows that his final design, when reproduced, must be 2″ x 3″. But he wishes to make his inked rendering larger in scale so that any irregularities of line or fuzziness of edges will be less evident when the plate is reduced to the 2″ x 3″ size. He knows, also, that the inked rendering must not only be larger in size but also have the same proportion. Therefore, if a line is drawn diagonally from corner to corner and projected outward, any rectangle which would be formed with this diagonal line bisecting the corner would be the same proportion as the 2″ x 3″ form. (See diagram in Fig. 2-9.)

The interior designer should be especially conscious of scale in selecting furnishings for a room. More will be discussed later in this chapter on the problem of using scale to create optical illusions. At this point we are concerned primarily wtih the use of scale to create beautiful proportions. A large, bulky piece of furniture is not necessarily comfortable because of its size. Chairs which are small in scale, thin of line, may be especially comfortable due to the use of foam rubber under the upholstery. Several large, bulky pieces of furniture in a small room may appear entirely too large in scale, whereas the same number of pieces in smaller scale might give a very pleasing effect.

In costume design our sense of rightness demands that articles of apparel worn together should not show too great a difference in size relationship to the wearer and to each other. This size relationship might be applied to separate parts of the ensemble, such as the hat, bag, jewelry, fur scarf, or collar—all consistent with the scale of the wearer. It would also apply to the individual parts within the garment, such as the collar, cuffs, pockets, sleeves, trimming details or surface patterns and textures of fabrics in relation to the size of the wearer and to each other. A dainty young lady would be overburdened with a large picture hat and a purse the size of a shopping bag.

In choosing sizes of objects for an arrangement, such as a grouping of pictures on a wall, accessories on a table or open shelf, or parts of a centerpiece, a fine sense of proportion and scale must be considered. The ability to select harmony of size without either too much likeness or unlikeness—a pleasing difference—cannot be achieved in a day. Constant observation and experimentation with a variety of sizes leads one to an ever-broadening awareness of beautiful proportions. (See large and small scale designs in Figs. 2-10 and 11.)

DIVISION OF SPACE

One of the most important problems faced by the designer is that of organizing the total area into fine space relations. Pleasing proportions, mentioned earlier in this chapter, should have some quality of "strangeness." It should not be too evident that a space is divided in halves, or thirds, or quarters. On the other hand, neither should the divisions be so unusual that they are difficult to understand and appreciate.

Fig. 2-12.

When dividing a space or a line into two parts, like the above, placing the division close to B would probably be more satisfactory than placing the division exactly at B. Therefore, the space would not be divided exactly in the ratio of 2:3.

When dividing a space into two parts, the student should avoid dividing the spaces into two equal parts. If both subparts are the same, then interest is lost and there is a danger of boredom. The design must attempt to develop two parts that achieve interest and are still related. (See Fig. 2-14.)

In example B although a great amount of contrast has been created between the two shapes, the contrast becomes difficult to handle successfully. Great contrast may be used to produce a dramatic feeling. However, the new student must be careful that this does not become comical or grotesque. Mutt and Jeff are the classic examples of the great contrast in shapes used to create humor. Example C illustrates a more interesting division of space.

Division of space into more than two parts might involve repetition of spaces, variation of spaces, or a combination of repetition with variety. The fewer divisions of space, the greater the variety there may be. (See Fig. 2-13.)

Division of space both horizontally and vertically may be done mathematically, planning progressively larger or smaller areas as in the whirling square. Or the eye may be used as a guide in creating a variety of areas which seem to harmonize or contrast with each other in a satisfying manner.

Diagonal lines create a dynamic effect in a composition. One should

Fig. 2-13. A. Monotonous division of spaces—all the same size. B. Variety of spacing—each one is different. C. Gradation of spacing—small to large. D. Variation of spacing—narrow light spaces, wide dark spaces. E. Variation of spacing—narrow dark spaces, wide light spaces. F. Gradation of spacing —small to large in both light and dark.

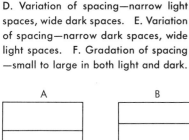

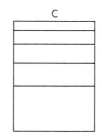

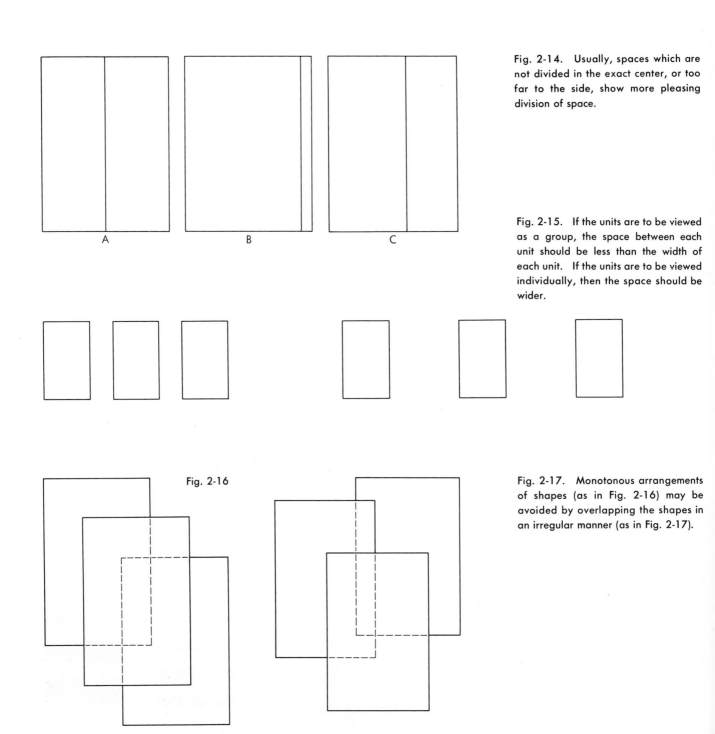

Fig. 2-14. Usually, spaces which are not divided in the exact center, or too far to the side, show more pleasing division of space.

A   B   C

Fig. 2-15. If the units are to be viewed as a group, the space between each unit should be less than the width of each unit. If the units are to be viewed individually, then the space should be wider.

Fig. 2-16

Fig. 2-17. Monotonous arrangements of shapes (as in Fig. 2-16) may be avoided by overlapping the shapes in an irregular manner (as in Fig. 2-17).

Fig. 2-18 (*Top*). The shapes show a pleasing variation in shape, size, height, dark, and light.

Fig. 2-19 (*Bottom*). The shapes show variation in shape and in dark and light, but are all too much the same height for pleasing arrangement in proportion.

be careful, however, not to direct one's attention more to a specific corner than to the structural shape.

Frequently, the grouping of objects, such as pictures on a wall, items on a counter, or repeat-units in a border, cause one to consider the amount of space to be left between each object or motif. A good general rule to follow might be: if the objects are to be enjoyed individually, then the space between can be greater than the amount of space occupied by the single unit. If, however, the objects or motifs are to be viewed as a group, then the space between should be less than that occupied by the unit. Consider the stepping stones in a path. If the stones are further apart than the size of the stone so that one has to jump from one stone to the next, such an arrangement does not enable one to walk easily along the path. (See Fig. 2-15.)

If objects are overlapped in an arrangement, then a variation in the space overlapped might lend more pleasing relationships in proportion. (See Fig. 2-16.)

CREATING OPTICAL ILLUSIONS

To suggest a change in appearance of an area by means of proportion might involve the lengthening or broadening effects of vertical and horizontal lines. In general, we usually say that lines running in a vertical direction tend to slenderize and make an object appear taller, whereas lines running in a horizontal direction would make an object appear shorter and broader. There are exceptions to nearly all "rules," however. It is quite possible that a fabric with narrow to medium stripes used horizontally the full length of a straight sheath-type garment worn by a short, slender figure might tend to create the illusion of height due to the fact that the lines are short horizontally and are extended over a relatively long space from hem to shoulder. If, however, the figure were plump, as well as short, and the stripes were broad, the emphasis would be more on the horizontal direction of the stripes rather than on the illusion of height because of the repetition of the stripes. The reverse of this example would be true with vertical stripes.

We are all familiar with the diagrams where diagonal lines may be used

25

to make a line appear shorter or longer. This principle may be used to advantage in costume design to change the apparent height of a figure by features such as collars, raglan sleeves, necklines, kick pleats, yokes, pockets, seams, or trimming details.

Scale may play an important role in creating optical illusions. In a small room many large or heavy pieces of furniture, figured upholstery, drapery, wallpaper, or floor covering may reduce the apparent size of the room. But place in the same room thin-line furniture, large areas of solid colors, light in value, grayed in intensity with small accents of bright intensities or dark values, and the room will appear much larger. The reverse would be true if one wished to make the room appear smaller. The one exception might be to concentrate more on large areas of low values and grayed intensities rather than on large areas of bright intensities. The large area of bright intensity would reduce the apparent size of the room, but would no doubt be difficult to live with for any length of time because it would be contrary to the "Law of Areas" as discussed later in the chapter on color.

An entire design must be visualized in order to be able to evaluate the principle of proportion correctly. Each part is dependent upon every other part. One part may appear correct when seen by itself but seem entirely out of proportion when seen with other parts of the design. (See Fig. 2-23.)

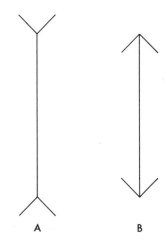

Fig. 2-20. The vertical lines are the same length, but the diagonal lines in A create the optical illusion of additional length. The diagonal lines in B create the optical illusion of reducing the length.

BALANCE

Balance is the principle of design that gives a feeling of repose due to the illusion of equal tensions or weights on both sides of the composition. Formal or symmetrical balance may be bisymmetrical or obvious. In other words, same or similar units on each side of the design should be placed equal distances from the center. The fact that the units are the same or similar will indicate that they give the *impression* of equal weights. (See Fig. 2-28A.) Therefore, if they are placed the same distances from the center, they will automatically be balanced. This takes for granted, of course, that the upper and lower portions of the design are so arranged as to give a feeling of balance. Thus there is not the effect of too much

Fig. 2-21. A graceful, rhythmical design, such as that in the armchair, is made possible today because of the use of molded plywood.

Fig. 2-22. A beautifully proportioned lamp with well-designed border decorations. A well-proportioned table with pleasing grain lines. Are they harmonious when used together?

Fig. 2-23. When we add the chair, are the three pieces harmonious with each other? (Lamp, The Charles Co., Inc. Table, designed by William Paul Taylor for Selected Designs, Inc., Beverly Hills, California. Chair, Paul McCobb.)

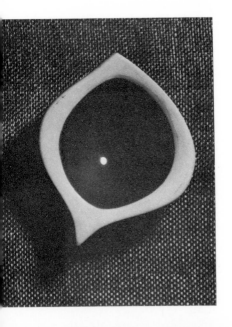

(upper left)
Fig. 2-24. An irregular shape for a ceramic ash tray with irregular thickness of the sides expresses imagination and pleasing proportions. (Made by Howard Kilns, Staten Island, New York.) (Photograph courtesy of Raymor Manufacturing Division.)

(upper right)
Fig. 2-25. Spaces which are divided off-center stimulate interest.

(lower left)
Fig. 2-26. Three sizes of the same shape provide greater possibilities for pleasing arrangements. (Designed by Val Robbins.) (Photograph courtesy of Jaru Art Products, Inc.)

(lower right)
Fig. 2-27. Unlike, but harmonizing, forms for salt and pepper shakers give variety and provide a "conversation piece." (Photograph courtesy of Design Today, Inc.)

weight at the bottom or a top-heavy appearance. For instance, a dark ceiling may be used to advantage in a room with a high ceiling, but a dark blouse and light skirt would make a short person look even shorter.

Formal balance is sometimes referred to as a passive or static balance because of the quiet dignity or stateliness and formality that is evident in its organization. Designs which are stately are sometimes quite active or dynamic in their impressions, however. A steeply sloped roof on a church may have an active, moving quality about it which cannot be denied.

The inexperienced person who is not aware of beautiful space variations may not at first succeed in creating a satisfactory example of formal balance, although it is relatively easy to center a picture, a doorway, or a flower arrangement for a centerpiece. One must be sensitive, however, to the ways in which one can employ the principle of formality so that the end result will not be trite and uninteresting.

In planning an informally balanced design, one has many more items to consider: the size and number of forms grouped on either side of the center; the distance from the center or the distance from the front or back of a design that each form is placed; or the way in which the dark and light, bright or dull, warm and cool forms of colors are used to give a proper feeling of balance.

The diagrams of the scales may explain the principle of balance, especially in the placement of shapes in a design. In Fig. 2-28A the shapes are the same in size, shape, and value of dark and light. They are placed the same distance from the center and thus express formal bisymmetrical balance. In B the two shapes on the right (when combined) have the same weight as the one on the left. Thus, they also are placed the same distance from the center and give a variation of formal balance which is not so monotonous. In C the object on the left is much larger than the one on the right, but because it is so light in value, it can be placed the same distance from the center as the dark shape and still give the impression of equal weights on both sides. This also is a variation of formal balance.

In D the large and small shapes are both dark, showing the impression of heaviness of the larger one so it pulls the scales down on the right. In E, by shifting the smaller shape to the left and bringing the larger shape

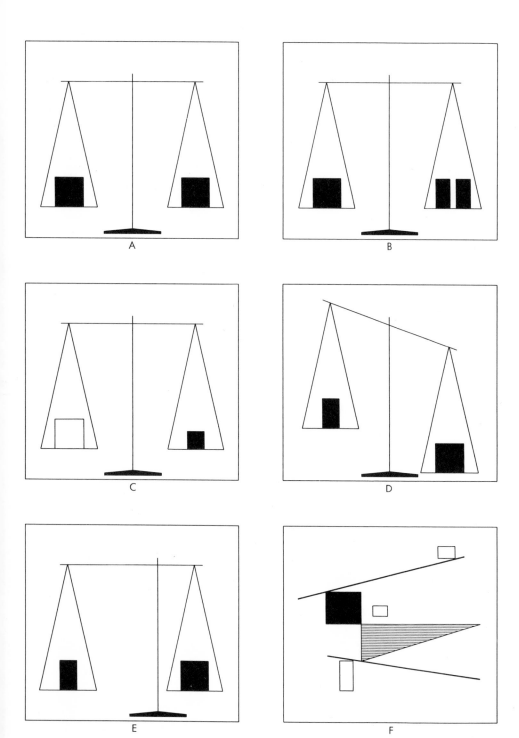

Fig. 2-28. Diagrams of types of balance.

closer to the center, proper informal balance is achieved.

In these examples we see what happens when "actual weights" are used, whereas in most art problems we are concerned more with creating *optical illusions* of equal weights. A number of different factors may cause a form to *appear* more heavy: size, color, texture, decorative pattern, or placement. Automatically, the unit which is made large in size will appear heavier. Actually, it might be constructed of a type of material which would literally make it weigh less than a small object. For instance, a block of balsa wood which is 4″ x 4″ at the base and 10 inches high might weigh less than a block of ebony which is 2″ x 2″ at the base and 6 inches high. It is the association that we have with size that causes us to *imagine* that the larger object is heavier. If one were planning a composition where the viewer was not going to handle the various parts of the design, the visual appearance only would be used as a guide in organizing the elements so that they appeared well balanced.

In F a variety of lines and shapes in varying degrees of darkness and lightness has been arranged in a complex informally balanced design. We need to use the eye as a gage in shifting the parts around in the composition to determine whether they *appear* to be balanced. We cannot put them on a scale and weigh them.

In general, we associate warmer colors, brighter intensities, and darker values with a feeling of more weight. Therefore, we would plan to arrange the units of the design so the form of the colors could be utilized to advantage in determining the correct balance. The heavier forms of colors would be used in smaller areas or closer to the center, or in the lower parts of the design. If it is a three-dimensional design, the heavier forms of colors would no doubt be placed further from the front.

Informal or asymmetrical balance is sometimes referred to as active or dynamic because of the variety of ways in which an area may be organized. It is more difficult for the person untrained in art to develop a sensitivity for the beautiful casual spontaneity expressed in informal balance. Actually, when we view a room in which there is a functional arrangement of a storage piece beside a desk, or a table and lamp beside a chair, or any other arrangement planned for use, we can see a reason for not having identical forms on both sides of the design. But when we see a picture placed off-center in a wall space or a flower arrangement

(upper left)
Fig. 2-29. A hand-blown vase of Orefors crystal expresses formal balance in the colored glass center with the thick, clear glass of the outer part. (Photograph courtesy of Zacho, Inc.)

(upper right)
Fig. 2-30. A cut-paper clown design shows bisymmetrical formal balance with the two halves that are identical.

(lower left)
Fig. 2-31. A screen-printed scroll *suggests* formal balance, although close scrutiny shows a slight difference in the design of the two birds. (Photograph courtesy of Design Today, Inc.)

(lower right)
Fig. 2-32. *Suggested* formal balance in the details of the head of the paper-sculptured animal are made more interesting by the slight variation of the placement of the ears and mouth.

Fig. 2-33. *Almost identical carving on each side of the wooden sculptured figure relieves the monotony of bisymmetrical formal balance.* (Designer, W. J. Westenhaver, Art Director for Witco, Inc.)

which is high on one side and low on the other, there may be present that quality of strangeness which is difficult at first to appreciate fully. We cannot "see" how the design achieves its equilibrium. But the unusual arrangement tends to arouse our curiosity and set us thinking.

During the last generation there have been many changes in our homes. There has been especially great change from formal living to the more informal. This difference is not only evident in ways we entertain but in the way we live. Informality has also moved into business and other walks of life. People working in group dynamics have discovered that discussion takes place better in an informal situation than when the leader stands at the head of a room and all of the furniture faces the front. Informal situations have shown us that we feel more at ease, feel more a part of what is going on in informal situations.

This stress on informality has influenced the designer, or maybe vice versa. In most situations we feel that informal design may create more dramatic situations. The design that is planned with informal design, then, has become more accepted and a part of present-day living. Each designer must decide if he wishes to produce formal or informal design. This decision must depend on the use of his design, as well as on the personality of the designer.

As a new design student, you must also become sensitive to the fact that informal design is not just scattering the design haphazardly. Often the person who has not developed sensitivity to informal design may be guilty of making his design a hodge podge. You must develop an awareness to both approaches to balance and then decide which you will use in each design problem. (See Figs. 2-29 to 38.)

EMPHASIS

Every design needs some note of interest that catches the eye or arrests the attention. This quality may be referred to as the *center of interest*, *point of emphasis*, or *dominant area*. It involves the principle of design which leads the eye first to the most important part of the design and then to other subordinating areas in the order of their importance. It is implied that there will be several centers of interest—which is true—although one

33

will be more dominant than the others and will arrest the attention longer and draw the eye back to itself more frequently than will the lesser centers of interest. Otherwise, there would be competing areas of emphasis which would no doubt cause confusion.

WHAT TO EMPHASIZE

We need to be aware of the many possibilities of what to emphasize. In a room arrangement, a window area, a grouping of sofa, tables, and accessories, or a fireplace wall might have attention directed toward them. In an ensemble, an unusual construction arrangement of seams or interesting decorative detail, or a beautiful accessory, such as a hat, scarf, or bag, might be made the center of attraction. It might easily be one way of drawing attention away from an undesirable figure irregularity.

HOW TO EMPHASIZE

There are several ways in which we may attract attention to the important part of a design. Some of these are:

1. By use of contrasts of hue, value, or intensity
2. By leading lines
3. By unusual detail
4. By grouping or placing of objects

Sometimes several of these methods might be combined in a single design.

The eye is quickly attracted by strong contrast of dark and light, bright and dull, or by contrasts of hue if they are also decidedly different in value. Bright red letters on a bright blue background would be contrasting in hue but would vibrate too much and be difficult to read because of their close value relationship. But if dark red letters were used on a light blue background they would still be contrasting in hue, and would be much easier to read because of the lack of vibration. The dark red would command more attention, whereas the light blue would be subordinated to it.

One is also conscious of the heaviness of **boldface** type as compared to

34

Fig. 2-34. The variation in thickness of the glass in the Orefors vase provides a pleasant example of informal balance. (Photograph courtesy of Zacho, Inc.)

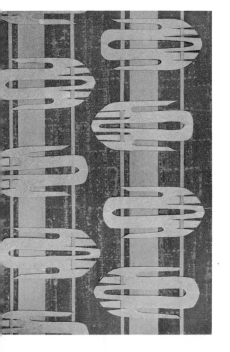

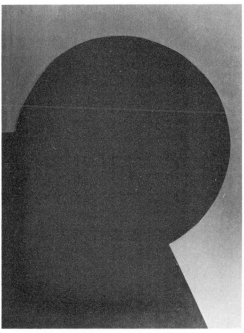

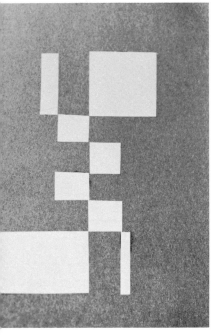

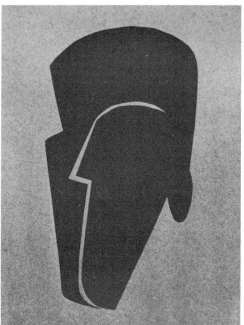

(upper left)
Fig. 2-35. A cut-paper all-over repeat suggests a feeling of formal balance. The interlacing lines and half-drop repeat add variety.

(upper right)
Fig. 2-36. A large area of dark may be balanced by a smaller area of light, or vice versa.

(lower left)
Fig. 2-37. The square and heavy rectangle at the top balance informally the larger rectangle and thin one at the bottom of the design.

(lower right)
Fig. 2-38. The cut-paper design shows the high cheek bone on one side balancing informally the large lobe of the ear on the other side.

lightface to call attention to a phrase or paragraph. Especially in advertising for magazines, posters, or display purposes, lines are employed in different ways to direct one's attention to centers of interest. In a magazine advertisement or poster, lines of various widths may break up the background space and lead the eye to the most important and then to lesser points of interest and also give a decorative quality to the advertisement. For display purposes, rods, paper streamers, ribbons, and various other materials may be used to advantage to give a line effect to draw the attention to a particular part of the display. In our discussion of the principle of proportion we mentioned the advisability of using lines in this way so that they would direct one's attention to the important part of the arrangement rather than to the corners of the page or window.

No doubt we have all had the experience of passing by a window where was displayed an unusual color, suit, picture, or accessory to which we turned to give a second and longer look. The fact that it was not the usual color to which we were accustomed, or the typical convertible collar on the suit, or the familiar scene in the picture was cause enough for us to be attracted more strongly to the unusual. This quality of unusualness may be one of beauty or grotesqueness, an amusing caricature, or unusual size, shape, or texture, or decorative pattern. The fact that it is something out of the ordinary is sufficient to attract our attention to it and make it seem important.

A dynamic character due to the compact arrangement of a number of items in a group may be more effective than if each part were displayed by itself. A rhythmic quality of leading one's attention in a progressive manner to the important part of a composition requires a definite awareness of beautiful proportions. We use the term "center of interest" with no intention of placing the emphasis literally in the center. By placing it a bit to the right or left of center, and a bit above or below the center we arrive at a much more effective location for the main "point" of emphasis. In progressing easily to other subordinated areas of interest and arriving back again at the dominant one requires a "path" over which the eye may travel in an easily connected manner. The problem is not to place the least dominant center of interest so near the edge of a composition that it will be likely to lead the attention *out* of the picture rather than back to the main area of attraction. (See Fig. 2-39A and B.)

36

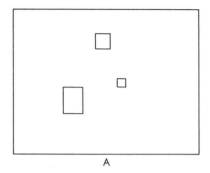

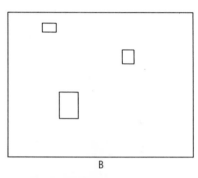

Fig. 2-39. The three centers of interest should be so arranged that the eye is carried easily from the most important to the least, and vice versa. In B the least important leads the eye out of the design.

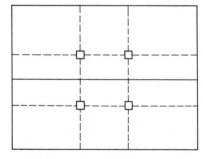

Fig. 2-40. The main center of interest should usually be located a bit above or below, a bit to the right or to the left of the center, horizontally and vertically.

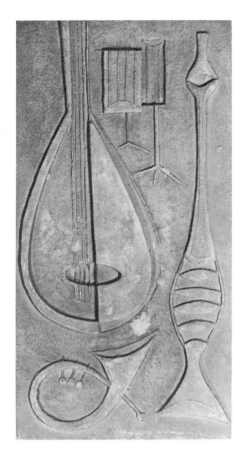

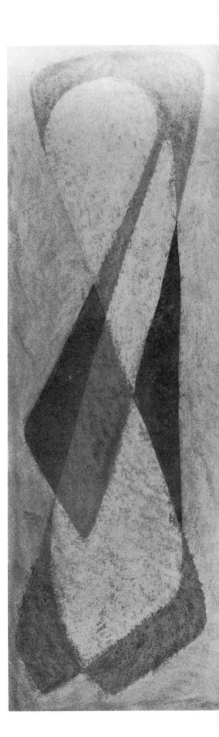

(extreme right)
Fig. 2-41. The main emphasis is on the two-value diamond shape on the left, then on the dark triangle on the right, and finally to the irregular shapes at the top and bottom.

(upper left)
Fig. 2-42. The main emphasis is on the mandolin on the left because of its larger size. (Photograph courtesy of Design Today, Inc.)

(lower left)
Fig. 2-43. The curved points in the lower part of the design lead the eye in a circular path to the black and white ovals as the center of attraction.

Mounting a picture on a background shape or planning a mat for it are problems in proportion, balance, and in emphasis. One needs to plan the width of margins to be pleasing in relation to each other. The picture is to be viewed on the wall in a vertical position, and therefore one needs to plan the bottom margin wider than the other three for better balance. If they were all the same, the "Law of Optics" would make the picture appear to be sliding down in space. From the standpoint of emphasis, we need a rectangular shape of background on which to place the rectangular picture in order to emphasize the picture and not the background. If a rectangular picture were placed on an oval background, they would both be competing for attention. If the object is to be viewed in a flat position or from all sides like a tablecloth on a table, then the opposite sides should be the same size and should be parallel with the table. Placing a cloth in a diagonal manner on a table is contrary to the shape of the table and there is lack of emphasis on the cloth in relation to the table.

RHYTHM

A sense of order, a quality of gracefulness, a feeling of easy movement— all lead to a principle of design which we may call "rhythm." All of us may tingle to the tips of our toes when we watch the graceful, lithe, movements of a ballet dancer as she pirouettes, spins, and leaps. If she appears clumsy in her movements, it may be because of lack of skill, but it also shows an absence of a feeling for beautiful *rhythmic* movement.

Rhythm, then, is not possible without this related movement or this sense of leading the eye easily from one part of a design to another in an easy, flowing manner. We say that a certain design shows rhythm, but it is not in the individual shapes, but in the change from one line to another, from one dimension to another, from one color to another, one value to another. In music, it isn't that each sound is rhythmical but in the change from one sound to another with the proper amount of time elapse between each note, or the change in pitch of each note. Sounds like a drum beat can become rhythmical when the beats are rapid at times and slow at others, arranged

Fig. 2-44. (*Top*) If an object is to be viewed from the top or from all sides, the margins are usually the same on opposite sides, and the object harmonizes in shape with the background shape. (*Bottom*) If an object is to be viewed in a vertical position, the bottom margin is usually wider than the other three.

in a semblance of order or a "certain time." On the other hand, the notes might be all timed the same, but they may vary in pitch.

1. **Repetition.** We may express a feeling of rhythm by *repetition* of lines, colors, and shapes, but in so doing we must also keep in mind the principles of proportion which deal with unity, with a certain amount of variety to add interest. (See Figs. 2-45 to 47.) Lines that are all the same length and thickness with the same spacing between each would give us an example of repetition, but it might be very monotonous. Properly organized lines or shapes for a background for wallpaper, all-over fabric design, or floor covering might show a definite regular repeat in order to keep the design "in the background." But a design for a more dramatic effect, as in a room-divider, may show more irregularity of spacing for pleasing rhythm.

2. **Gradation or Progression.** A gradual change in the length or thickness of lines may give variety, but if it is so obvious that one is striving for *gradation* or *progression,* it, too, would become monotonous. Besides a gradual change in length or thickness of lines, one may seek variety in a change in spacing between lines, or shapes; change in hue, value, or intensity; change in amounts overlapped in a composition; change in texture from smooth to rough, shiny to dull. (See Figs. 2-48 to 50.)

3. **Continuous Related Movement.** In some designs it is not evident that any elements are repeated, or that there is a progressive change from one part of the design to another, and yet we have a sense of easy movement throughout the design. This related movement may be literally in a *continuous line.* It may be in a *suggestion* of a continuous line, occasionally having breaks in the line but spaces that are small enough so the eye still carries over to the next section of the line in a rhythmical manner. (See Fig. 2-51.) The movement may be in a series of lines within lines as in growth rings of a tree trunk or grain lines in a plank of wood. We may call this "continuous related movement" which produces a feeling of rhythm. In the flowing lines of an Oriental garment we may see a beautiful example of continuous related movement throughout the entire garment.

We usually think of rhythm as expressing a quality of lithesome grace, but this does not exclude the rapid, dramatic, sharp slashes of a Voodoo dancer or the rapid zigzag of a lightning flash. These express other kinds of rhythm which show more speed, but they might still express repetition,

(upper left)
Fig. 2-45. Shapes may be repeated, but they may make a rather monotonous arrangement if they are all the same size and same distance apart.

(lower left)
Fig. 2-46. Even though the shapes are identical, they can give a more pleasing rhythmical pattern when the spaces between them are varied.

(upper right)
Fig. 2-47. Besides having the spaces varied between shapes, other decorative details, such as the thin and heavy lines, might be added.

(left)
Fig. 2-48. A more subtle gradation in size, and dark and light have been used in the "Forest" with a different decorative design planned for each tree. (Designer, Ethel Jane Beitler.)

(upper right)
Fig. 2-49. Shapes may be graduated in size, but when they are much the same in shape and the gradation is too obvious, the design becomes monotonous.

(lower right)
Fig. 2-50. A more dramatic effect can be produced by more subtle gradation.

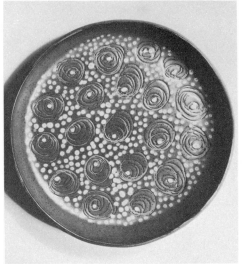

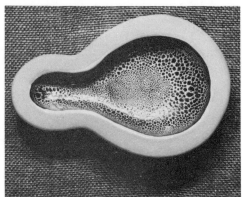

(left)

Fig. 2-51.   The terra cotta wall plaque expresses rhythm by means of a beautiful continuous line movement throughout the design.   (Photograph courtesy of Design Today, Inc.)

(upper right)

Fig. 2-52.   The designer of a ceramic ash tray playfully uses repetition for a rhythmical all-over pattern.   Photograph courtesy of Marshall Studios, Inc.   Designers: Jane and Gordon Martz.

(lower right)

Fig. 2-53.   The "iron spots" in the glaze of the base of the ceramic ash tray express a subtle gradation of size, creating a rhythmical pattern.   (Designer, Harding Black.   Photograph courtesy of Design Today, Inc.)

Fig. 2-54. The variation in height of the figures in the foreground and the dark spires of the Cathedral in the background create a graceful rhythm throughout the tapestry. ("Cathedral," tapestry designed by Martta Taipole. Photograph courtesy of the American Craftsmen's Council.)

Fig. 2-55. The gradation of size of the triangles of white walrus tusk and the continuous line movement of the grain of the wood lead the eye in a rhythmical manner. Wood carving by George Federoff. (Photograph courtesy of the American Craftsmen's Council.)

gradation, or continuous related movement.

Some designers will include a fifth principle of design, that of *harmony*. It is the opinion of the authors that if the principles of proportion, balance, emphasis, and rhythm are applied creatively so that there is a sense of beauty in the design, the resulting attribute will be that of harmony or unity. It is a culminating goal toward which we are striving when we select and arrange the various elements of design for a particular purpose. If we have failed to apply any one of the principles of design, then the resulting design will also lack harmony.

Let us use a particular design (that in Fig. 2-48) to consider the ways in which the various principles of design have been planned in relation to it. *Informal balance* has been used, with different "tree" shapes placed different distances from the center but so neither side seems to be heavier than the other nor have a greater power of attraction. Sufficient dark value and larger shapes have been used in the lower part to give a feeling of stability, and yet there is also some dark value in smaller amounts in the upper part to carry the eye upward and balance the whole composition.

Unity with variety in the *proportions* has been achieved. The "tree" shapes are all triangles, but they vary both in size and in the decorative manner in which the space is broken in each one. *Emphasis* has been placed on the small figures of the elk by making them dark in value and surrounding them with a light background. The "trees" are also clustered around them to center attention on them. *Rhythm* has been attained by means of repetition, gradation, and continuous line movement. There is gradation of size of the triangular shapes from the small ones at the top to the large ones at the base. They have the same basic shape, even though each "tree" has a different decorative pattern of "branches." A feeling of continuous line movement has been achieved by overlapping the shapes in differing amounts so the eye is led in a rhythmical path from one shape to the next. The straight lines of the "trunks" also lead the eye from the base of the panel to the top. The composition lends itself to its use as a decorative wall panel. Thus, because all the principles of design have been applied appropriately, we can assume there is *harmony* in the composition. The lack of harmony would enter into the problem if one used this design inappropriately as a wall panel with formal traditional furnishings. It suggests an informal contemporary setting.

It is true that too much "academic" evaluation of a design can sometimes cause the design to become stiff and lacking in spontaniety. A design is not necessarily good just because we set out to deliberately achieve balance, pleasing proportion, or locate a center of interest. It must be the result of much searching, experimentation, and many trials. The final design may appear to have been done quickly and with little effort, but it takes as much practice and skill as a musician would use in learning to play a concerto.

Under the pretense of harmony one can carry an idea to the extreme. For instance, it is possible to carry association of ideas so far that it becomes ridiculous, as when a steak platter is decorated with a bright red steak or a preserve jar is shaped like a strawberry with a cluster of leaves and a stem for the handle. Our problem is to train ourselves to recognize the significant and creative from the commonplace and faddish.

Our tastes are developed through study, observation, association, and experience. In a course such as this book suggests, we are exposed to a discussion of terms pertaining to design. We experience the opportunity of creating designs ourselves and observing demonstrations or watching techniques with which fellow classmates experiment. Thus we grow in our sensitivity toward the organization of the principles of design so that the resulting attribute will be *harmony*.

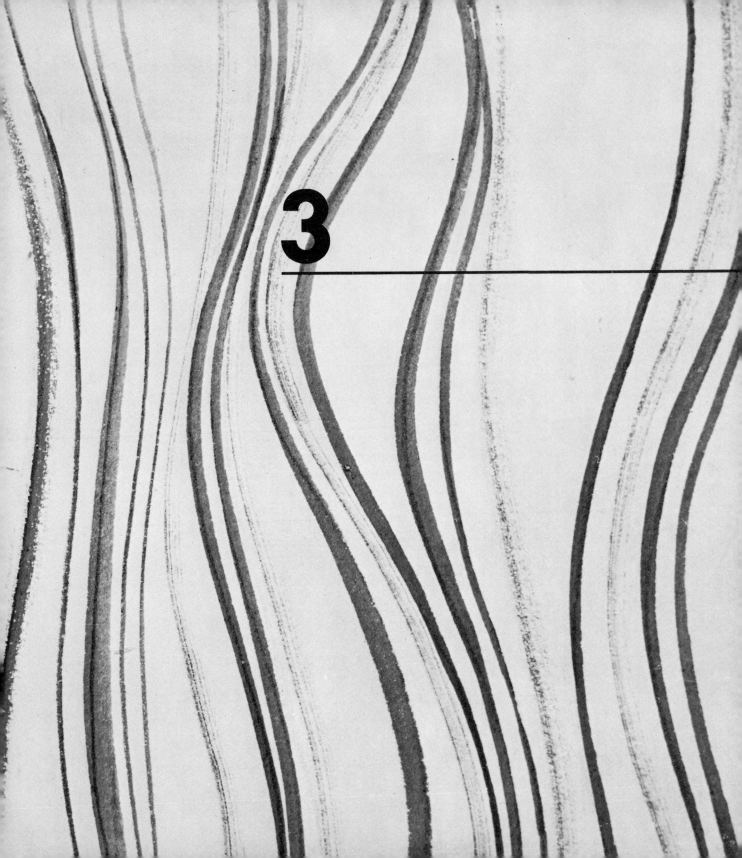

WHAT'S YOUR LINE?

On a piece of paper we make a mark that causes our eyes to move from one end of the mark to the other. We call such a mark a "line." Rathbun and Hayes in *Layman's Guide to Modern Art* state: "Line is an abstraction; there are boundaries but no actual lines in nature. Objects merely come to an end and other objects begin, but the painter represents this fact by a line." Line has only one major dimension—length—but may move in any direction. The width or thickness of line may introduce a second dimension. However, it is debatable as to how thick a line may be before it becomes identified as a shape.

All lines fall into the category of straight, curved, or a combination of these two. This may produce wavy, scalloped, or zigzag lines. Lines can basically move in a vertical, horizontal, or diagonal direction, or a combination of any of these. (See Fig. 3-4.) Physical characteristics of lines may be described as thick, thin, smooth, fuzzy, long, short, as well as many others. The various tools, materials, and techniques used to create lines will help determine these physical characteristics. (See photographs on pages 62 to 64 for examples of experiments with lines, using a variety of tools, materials, and techniques.) The emotional quality of the line may be defined as exciting, quiet, dignified, angry, active, or happy. The emotional quality of a line is the result of its direction and physical qualities as interpreted by the designer.

47

Fig. 3-1. The graceful stream of white vapor trail from a jet plane as it whizzes into the air suggests to the long-range viewer a diminishing line quality. (Photograph U. S. Air Force.)

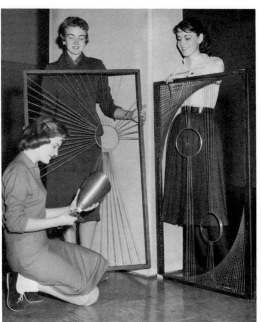

(lower left)
Fig. 3-2. The desk and chair, designed by George Nelson for the Herman Miller Furniture Company, suggest a delicate linear quality. The fabric, designed by Alexander Girard, suggests a free, broken line which harmonizes with the furniture.

(lower right)
Fig. 3-3. Cord, wire, and embroidery hoops make exciting line-dividers for display purposes.

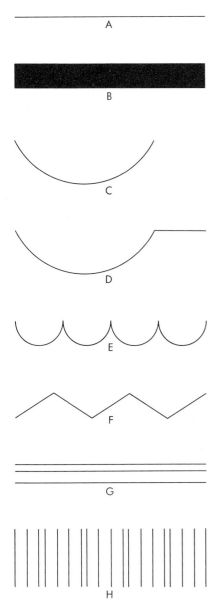

Fig. 3-4. A. Straight line. B. Is it a line or a shape? C. Curved line. D. Straight and curved lines combined. E. Scalloped line. F. Zigzag line. G. Horizontal lines. H. Vertical lines.

In order to enjoy life to the utmost, one needs to be continually observing with rapt attentiveness even the smallest details of his environment. If we have trained ourselves to notice, we will be more inclined to notice everything—not just the design of a garment and the color and texture of the fabric, but the least irregularity of hemline, or unevenness of stitching in a seam. Of course we will note not only the unsatisfactory items but also the many points of beauty. We mentioned earlier that "there are boundaries but no actual lines in nature." However, if we regard a scene from nature with attention, we begin to see where lines are *suggested* by the curving waves, the rolling hills, or waving grain. We could put a sheet of tracing paper over a photograph of a natural form and sketch a pattern of lines. These suggestions of lines are everywhere about us if we will only open our eyes and enjoy their beauty. Following are only a few examples:

1. The irregular, dashing lines made by the waves as they lap the shoreline.

2. The lines made by the branches of the trees as they reach upward toward the sky.

3. The undulating movements of waving grain and grasses as they sway in the breeze.

4. The lacy pattern of veins in a leaf.

5. The radiating lines made by a clump of iris leaves.

6. The lines cut into the snow from tire treads or the marks of the chains.

7. The pattern of lines in a picket fence, a venetian blind, a striped or plaid fabric.

8. The composition of vertical and horizontal lines made by the steel framework of a building under construction.

9. The suggestion of irregular parallel lines in the grain of a beautiful piece of wood.

10. The graceful stream of white vapor trail from a jet plane as it whizzes through space.

An individual can develop a sensitivity to the beauty of the element of line in unplanned design and design in nature. Then it would become easier to go one step further and create interesting line patterns of his own. There are times when a simple arrangement of thick and thin, long and

Fig. 3-5. Contemporary hand-thrown ceramic bowl, made by Ed and Mary Schier, appropriately enriched with a scratched pattern of lines. (Courtesy of the American Craftsmen's Council.)

(lower left)
Fig. 3-6. The elegant "Roulette" pattern of Arzberg porcelain shows graceful rhythm in the radiating lines. (Designer, Jean Luce.)

(lower right)
Fig. 3-7. The bold lines in the ceramic vase on the left show strong contrast with the more delicate lines which decorate the vase on the right. (Photograph courtesy of Raymor Mfg. Division.)

A   B

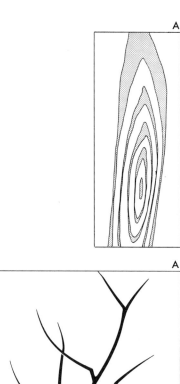 

Fig. 3-8A.   A line design inspired from the natural grain of wood shown in B.

A   B

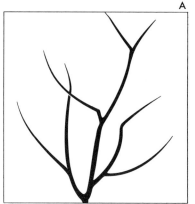 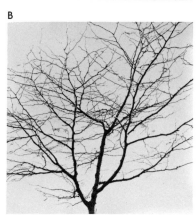

Fig. 3-9A.   A line design inspired from the natural radiation of branches of a tree shown in B.

A   B

Fig. 3-10A.   A line design inspired from the graceful leaves and plumes of pampas grass shown in B.

short, fuzzy and smooth will satisfy our need for decoration—just an interesting line pattern, with no attempt to represent an animal, a bird, or other object. It is sometimes wise to break away from the mathematically precise arrangement of lines which look as though each had been drawn with a ruler and the space between measured accurately. One of the secrets of the element of line is the recognition that it is possible to achieve beauty with a *planned* form of irregularity, rather than with the careless irregularity due to a lack of skill or planning. (Compare the preciseness or irregularity in Figs. 3-13, 14, and 15.)

One way in which lines might be classified includes:

1. Structural lines.
   a. To define a shape.
   b. To indicate a background.

2. Decorative lines.
   a. To form an all-over pattern or border.
   b. To express pure beauty of line, known as calligraphy.
   c. To express an emotional or physical quality.
   d. To create optical illusions.

S T R U C T U R A L   L I N E S

A. TO DEFINE A SHAPE

The most common form is that of the "outline." More on this point will be discussed later in the chapter on *Shape,* although here it might be stated that the shape of the object would be indicated by bringing the ends of the line together. For instance, a line may be curved so much that the opposite ends meet and form a circle or oval. (See Fig. 3-11.) Four lines the same length may be touched at the ends to form a square. (See Fig. 3-12.) From these simple illustrations we may go on to recognize the use of lines to define the shape of a human figure, an animal, a building, or any particular object. The degree to which these lines are exaggerated in length or direction may indicate the degree of abstraction or realism which may be represented in the design. (See Figs. 3-16, 17.)

52

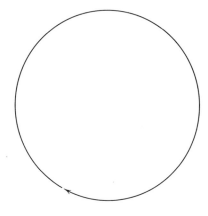

Fig. 3-11 (*Top*). Lines may be used to "define a shape." Bring the ends of a line together to make a circle.

Fig. 3-12 (*Bottom*). Bring the ends of four lines together to make a square.

Fig. 3-13. The exact or "ruler-precise" lines show variety in length, direction, and spacing.

Fig. 3-14. Freehand pen and ink lines show organization with pleasing variation in spacing but no exactness due to the use of a ruler.

Fig. 3-15. Freehand lines were made with a brush and tempera paint. Note the manner in which the lines have been organized in a "unit" and the unit repeated as a border.

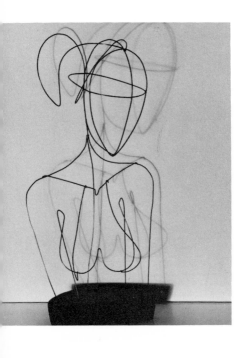

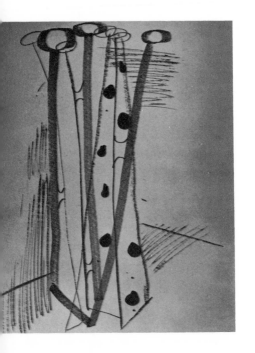

Fig. 3-16. The continuous length of copper wire is bent and welded together to suggest the female figure. No attempt has been made to represent in a realistic way the individual features of eyes, nose, mouth, hair, and yet there is no question of the intent of the designer to represent a female figure.

(upper right)
Fig. 3-17. Angular pen lines suggest buildings, hills, trees, boats, or whatever one wishes to imagine the lines represent. (Stuart Davis, Composition Number 4, 1934. Brush and Ink, Gift of Mrs. John D. Rockefeller, Jr. Courtesy of the Museum of Modern Art.)

(lower left)
Fig. 3-18. Thick and thin lines made with a felt pen suggest tall figures in a "corner." The corner is indicated by the angular lines near the base of the "figures."

(lower right)
Fig. 3-19. One might imagine a scene of castles beside a lakeshore with brush and trees on the right and white clouds overhead.

B. TO INDICATE A BACKGROUND

The shape which is represented by the lines will be further emphasized by means of other lines which may be used behind, in front, or beside the shape to suggest its relative position in space. Lines may suggest walls, floor, doorway, or stage, and therefore make the composition more meaningful. This does not mean, of course, that the walls, floor, doorway, or stage need be represented so realistically that there would be no doubt of their meaning. The lines could merely be used as a part of the background which in turn could be *interpreted* to suggest whatever the viewer wished to imagine. The lines would be used for the purpose of making the design more effective. (See Figs. 3-18, 19.)

DECORATIVE LINES

A. TO FORM A BORDER OR ALL-OVER PATTERN

The continuous beat of a drum with its rapid and slow, loud and soft reverberations of sound might suggest to us a pattern of lines which might be planned for a border. Many lines close together with an occasional one spaced further away could indicate the rapid and slow beats on the drum. Broad and short lines could suggest the loud and soft beats. And so, we develop a rhythmical border. (See Fig. 3-20.)

Repeating our border in all directions causes it to become an all-over pattern. If designers of wallpaper or printed fabrics had no other element except line, there still could be a never-ending array of arrangements that could be made. (See Fig. 3-21.)

B. TO EXPRESS PURE BEAUTY OF LINE, KNOWN AS CALLIGRAPHY

To some, the wrinkles that have developed in the brown and leathered face of a ninety-year-old grandmother mean nothing as far as age is concerned. They represent, rather, the beauty of lines that suggest the "living" which she has enjoyed over the years. The laugh lines radiating from the corners of the eyes and mouth, the anxiety lines in the forehead, the calligraphy of lines throughout her cheeks and chin—all express

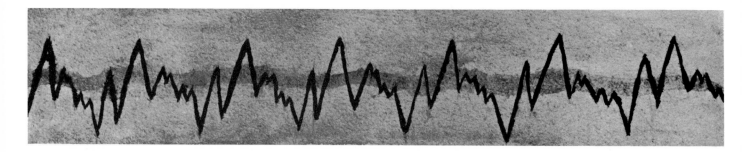

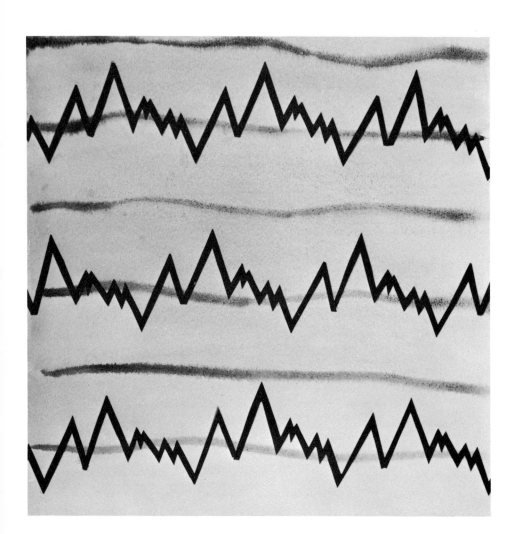

Fig. 3-20. A rhythmical border developed from the sound of an African drum beat.

Fig. 3-21. An all-over pattern developed from the border above.

Fig. 3-22. "The Dandelion," six feet tall, by Harry Bertoia, was not designed necessarily to resemble a dandelion but to be a spherical form which would enable one to look inside. The beautiful line pattern looks so fragile one might be afraid to touch it. (Owners, Mr. and Mrs. Harry Hood Bassett. Photograph by Herbert Matter. Reprinted from Vogue, Coypright 1959, The Condé Nast Publications, Inc.)

Fig. 3-23. The fragileness of the actual "dandelion gone to seed" also suggests a beautiful calligraphy of lines.

Fig. 3-24. The amusing charm of the few simple lines used by Paul Klee in his painting "Nearly Hit" produces a story of a narrow escape. (Photograph courtesy of San Francisco Museum of Art. Albert M. Bender collection.)

beauty of soul to those who love her.

The homeowner cannot help but be annoyed with the persistent growth of dandelions in his yard. But let a nice big one go to seed, and we must admit that the lacy, fuzzy lines suggested by the beautiful head is the most fragile calligraphy of lines imaginable. Harry Bertoia recognized that beauty when he created his six-foot sculpture of the "dandelion gone to seed." (See Figs. 3-22, 23.)

Occasionally an artist becomes more known for his line compositions than for any other quality. Paul Klee, for instance, has an amusing way with lines, making just a few of them express a mood or represent a child-like figure. (See Fig. 3-24.) Artzybascheff plays with continuous lines, twining and intertwining around each other in a rapid, rhythmical manner.

C. TO EXPRESS AN EMOTIONAL OR PHYSICAL QUALITY

Qualities of line may be described as:

1. Representational or descriptive.
2. Decorative or esthetic.
3. Emotional or suggestive.

The first quality, that of *representational or descriptive,* is a physical one to a large degree. For instance, if one were attempting to represent an object against a background, one could suggest a sense of space so much more effectively by using sharp lines in the foreground and fuzzy or wooly ones in the background.

When a line is used to define a shape, it may represent, in an abstract or realistic manner, some object with which we are familiar. There is sufficient "likeness" in the drawing for us to be able to use descriptive adjectives in relation to the lines. For instance, the lines may represent a fashion sketch. (See Fig. 3-25.) The lines enable us to determine the style of neckline, sleeves, fullness of the skirt, and general type of silhouette.

Decorative or *esthetic* qualities may be recognized in the details of the garment, as in the shape of the collar and the seam lines in the jacket. They may also be recognized in the beautiful spacing of lines between the seams. Esthetic qualities may also be discerned in a beautiful curved walk, a winding brook, drifting snow, or the sway of branches in the wind.

58

Fig. 3-25. In representing a fashion sketch, lines are made faint or thin on the side which shows highlights and made heavy on the shadow side. Lines enable us to determine the details of the garment. (Courtesy Lord & Taylor.)

Fig. 3-26.   Racehorse.

Fig. 3-27.   Workhorse.

Fig. 3-28.   Decorative horse.

Impressions of daintiness, boldness, or gracefulness may be *suggested* by fine lines, heavy lines, or curved ones respectively. In the fashion sketch referred to earlier the rendering has been developed with fine pencil strokes, expressing a quality of refinement. One might also note the easy, free quality expressed by the technique of the designer. Occasionally letting a line fade out, or leaving a blank space in the sketching of a line takes away the tightness or stiffness that might otherwise be expressed by means of a continuous contour line. The ends of the lines are close enough together that the eye can easily fill in the spaces. It may be compared to two lines that do not touch but suggest a right angle. When something is left to the imagination, the effect is more interesting than if all the details are complete. In listening to music, the occasional pause is more pleasing than the continuous sound of the melody. Our ears pick up the tune easily and go on.

Straight lines express stability. The fact that a line has no curves or bends in it indicates a forcefulness and strength necessary to keep it straight. When we lie down to rest, we assume a horizontal position; therefore, horizontal lines suggest repose and calmness. When we are standing or walking, we are in a vertical position, and consequently, vertical lines express activity. When we run, the legs, body, and arms assume more of a zigzag position, and the speed of running expresses more excitement and movement. The zigzag lines of lightning cannot help but make you tingle as you view the rapid irregular line of light in the sky.

These three ways of expressing emotional and physical qualities of line are quite evident in the three sketches of horses. (See Figs. 3-26, 27, 28.) In each sketch one can discern that a horse is *represented,* even though in an abstract manner. In the first sketch the lines are refined and are more delicate and sharp, *suggesting* the speed of a racehorse. In the second the lines are varied in thickness, but the predominance of thick lines *suggests* a heavy workhorse. The third is sketched in a highly *decorative* manner with a continuous line pattern to appeal to the esthetic emotions of the viewer. It shows a playful, fun-loving character on the part of the designer.

To be truly beautiful a line must appear to have some purpose. It must "go someplace" rather than meander aimlessly all over the space. The director of a large high school once cautioned his staff members, "If you find it necessary to leave your classrooms on an errand, walk as though you were going someplace with a purpose, and then if a board member or I happen to see you out of your classroom, we'll know it is a necessary absence from duty!" And so, with your lines—we can make them appear weak and uncertain of their destination, or we can make them strong, dynamic, and purposeful. (See Fig. 3-29A and B.)

Persons who make a study of handwriting like to suggest that it is possible to determine personality traits, state of one's health, criminal tendencies, and a host of other characteristics by the way in which we cross our "t's," shape our "m's," or run our letters together. The story is told that Abraham Lincoln, as he prepared to sign the Emancipation Proclamation, twice picked up his pen and put it down. Then he turned to William E. Seward, his Secretary of State, and said, "I have been shaking hands since nine o'clock this morning and my right arm is almost paralyzed. If my name ever goes into history, it will be for this act, and my whole soul is in it. If my hand trembles when I sign the Proclamation, all who examine the document hereafter will say, 'He hesitated.' "He then turned to the table, took up the pen again, and slowly, firmly, wrote, "Abraham Lincoln."

A

TO CREATE OPTICAL ILLUSIONS

Lastly we may use lines in a variety of ways to make things appear different from what they actually are. The student may refer back to Chapter 2 in the discussion of the principle of proportion and the problem of creating optical illusions by means of lines. In general, we say that horizontal lines add apparant width to a shape, and vertical lines tend to carry the eye up and down and add to the height. (See Fig. 3-30.)

It will be interesting for the student or others reading these chapters to find examples of lines or experiment with creating them, using as many different kinds of tools and materials as he has available. He may wish to find examples in actual objects such as string, grasses, sticks, wire, or clippings, or photographs. He may wish to play with pencil, pen, brush, string, or wire in creating his own interpretations. He may wish to make comparisons of qualities of line that are different, such as those produced with a fine pen and those made with a broad lettering pen; or a fine thread and a heavy rug yarn.

B

Fig. 3-29. A. An unorganized line design. B. An organized line design.

CREATIVE EXPERIMENTS

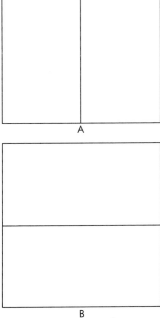

A

B

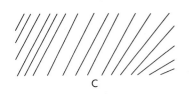

C

D

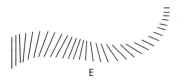

E

Following are exercises that are planned to help you as a student in your understanding and appreciation of the element of lines. The written information and illustrations should stimulate your ability to see and to create pleasing organizations of lines. Just reading these chapters and information in other sources cannot take the place of your continual observation and actual experimentation, using many techniques and a variety of tools and materials. You should constantly refer back, however, to the chapter on the principles of design to evaluate the arrangement of lines to determine if you have a feeling of proper balance, pleasing proportion, and effective emphasis, and graceful rhythm.

Nature offers us excellent keys to good organization in design. Man's reorganization of nature into stiff and regimented designs so often violates the natural beauty of nature. Frequently in landscaping of a garden the attempt is toward extreme formality which is in direct contrast to the pleasing informality of nature.

The following problems may help you to explore and become more aware of the characteristics of line.

1. Find examples of various types of lines in magazine illustrations. Ask yourself the following questions in evaluating the illustrations:
   a. In what ways do the lines reflect the character of the illustration?
   b. In what ways do the lines fail to reflect the character of the illustration?
   c. In what ways has variety been expressed in the lines? (Thickness, thinness, length of lines, direction of lines, straight vs. curved.)
   d. Does this variety of lines lead to a unified design?
   e. Does this variety of lines lead to discord or confusion?

Fig. 3-30. To create optical illusions: A. The vertical line tends to carry the eye up and down and lengthen the shape. B. The horizontal line tends to carry the eye across the figure and broaden the shape. C. The diagonal lines tend to make the right end appear to be wider. D. The straight lines emphasize the rhythm of a contour shape, such as a fence. E. The straight lines create the illusion of the fence standing up at the left end and lying down at the right end.

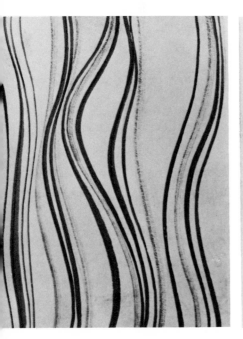

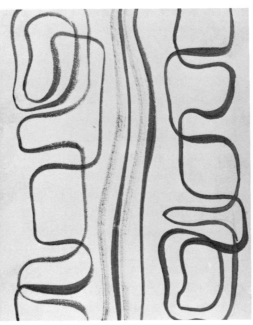

(upper left)
Fig. 3-31. Curved and straight lines were made with varying amounts of pressure put on the brush to give different widths of lines. Curved lines, not overlapping.

(upper right)
Fig. 3-32. Curved lines, with some continuous and overlapping.

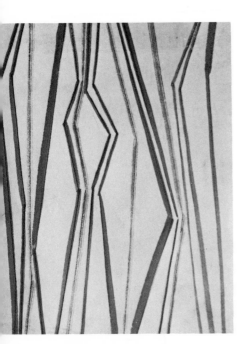

(lower left)
Fig. 3-33. Relatively straight and angular lines, with none overlapping.

(lower right)
Fig. 3-34. Relatively straight and angular lines, with some continuous and overlapping.

Fig. 3-35. A "scribbled" line design made with a felt pen held at the same angle to produce thick and thin lines. Less pressure was placed on the pen for the lines in the background to make them lighter in value.

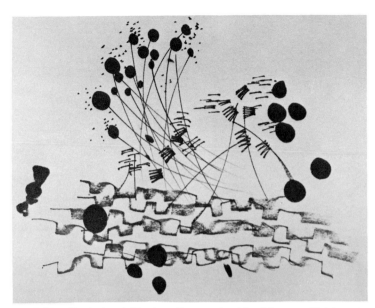

Fig. 3-36. Shaded and thin-sharp lines made with a felt pen, with ink spots for variation in dark and light.

Fig. 3-37. Rubber cement dripped on a light background and then covered with India Ink. When dry, the rubber cement was rubbed off to reveal the white lines.

Fig. 3-38. Lines made with a felt pen held flat for the solid lines and held on edge for the double lines. Lines were overlapped to create the optical illusion of interlacing.

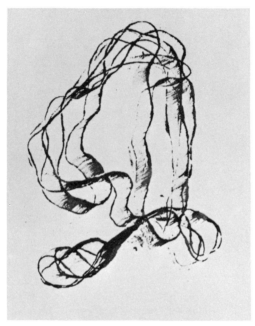

(upper left)
Fig. 3-39. Spatter painting can be relatively controlled to give a suggestion of a line pattern.

(upper right)
Fig. 3-40. A string dipped in paint and dropped onto a white or colored background creates a line pattern when covered with a second piece of paper. Shading results when the paper is moved slightly.

(lower left)
Fig. 3-41. India ink is painted over a piece of "scratch board." Freehand lines in graceful curves are scratched through the ink.

(lower right)
Fig. 3-42. Another India ink and scratch board technique, using all straight lines scratched along a ruler.

2. Find examples of suggestions of line in nature, such as veins in a leaf, grain of wood, or branches of a tree.

    a. Can you find an example in nature where exact repetition is evident?

    b. Can you find an example of variety which does not lead to unity?

3. Collect examples of actual materials which have a linear quality—paper clips, string, yarn, bamboo, matches, toothpicks, wire, etc.

The following experiments may help you to create your own designs with special emphasis on the element of line.

1. Make an assortment of kinds of lines—straight, curved, zigzag, wavy—with various tools such as pencil, pen, brush, crayon, chalk, tongue depressors, cord.

The photographs of designs shown in this chapter and others should not be expected to serve as models, but more as suggestions of the possibilities and limitations of particular tools and materials.

2. Move your hands in the air in a line pattern inspired by the rhythm of music. When you have a feeling for the rhythm, use chalk and develop a border design on paper. See Figs. 3-20 and 21 for examples of a rhythmical border and all-over pattern developed from the sound of an African drum beat. They were made with paint and cut paper. The timing of the beats and the tone quality of the musical sounds will automatically suggest to each individual a different arrangement of lines.

3. Work with tools in many ways—freehand, with a ruler, or using different amounts of pressure on the tool. In Figs. 3-31 to 34 a brush was used with varying amounts of pressure to produce different thicknesses of lines. Basically parallel, or continuous and overlapping lines, curved or relatively straight and angular lines produce continuous borders or repeats for all-over patterns. Some of the lines are dark because of the amount of paint in the brush, whereas others give a "dry-brush" effect. In Figs. 3-35 a felt pen was held at the same angle for the entire "scribbled" line design to produce thick and thin lines which have a different effect than the variation in thickness produced by different amounts of pressure on a pointed brush. In Fig. 3-38 a felt pen was held flat for some lines and on edge for other lines. Even the overlapping of lines creates the optical illusion of interlacing.

In Fig. 3-13 the lines are "ruler-precise," whereas in Fig. 3-14 the freehand pen and ink lines are organized in a pleasing variation in spacing but with no exactness because of the use of a ruler. In Fig. 3-15 the free-hand lines were made with a brush and tempera paint, organized as a unit and the unit repeated as a border. The lines go in a variety of directions and are painted with a free quality of irregularity of thickness, but the relative "straightness" of the lines give an orderly quality of harmonious unity.

4. Work with ink and paint in a variety of techniques on dry, damp, rough, and smooth backgrounds; crumpled paper, wax crayon resist, and scratch board. As in Fig. 3-37, rubber cement dripped on a white or colored background and then covered with India ink can produce a rhythmical line design if the rubber cement is thin enough to drip in a satisfactorily thick and thin manner. When dry the rubber cement can be rubbed off to reveal the line design. Sometimes additional lines can be scratched through the remaining black of the background for added decorative effect.

Scratchboard, which is available in most school supply stores, can be covered with India ink. This gives a satisfactory surface on which to scratch lines freehand as in Fig. 3-41 or along a ruler as in Fig. 3-42.

Some techniques are more difficult to control. In Fig. 3-39 the spatter painting technique was used. The paint was spattered in many directions for a textured background, but the brush can be loaded with paint and tapped against one's finger which is moved in a desired direction to give a relatively controlled suggestion of a line. If a string is dipped in paint or ink and organized on a background, it can be covered by a second piece of paper to produce an offset of the line design. By moving the paper slightly, shading or textural effects add interest to the line.

5. Make a border or all-over pattern with materials such as yarn, toothpicks, paper clips, or cut paper strips.

6. Think of words that could be expressed with line—anger, sadness, boldness, daintiness. Select a tool and a medium which you think would best express each word and create a pattern of lines. Try combining dainty with bold, angry with happy, to determine what factors are involved in using these combinations harmoniously together. In Fig. 3-43 the variation in thickness of brush strokes provides character and depth of emotion. In Fig. 3-46 a free brush and ink line expresses "depression" be-

Fig. 3-43. Variation in thickness of brush strokes provide character and depth of emotion. (Designer, Margaret Stites.)

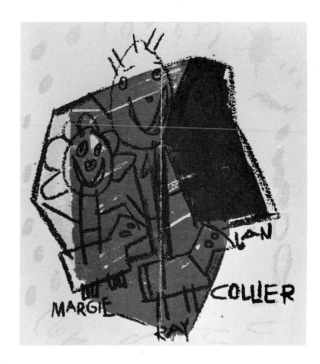

Fig. 3-44. A childlike, playful use of dry-brush lines for a personalized family greeting card. (Designer, Ray Collier.)

Fig. 3-45. The delicate "calligraphy" of line provides a decorative quality to the group of carolers.

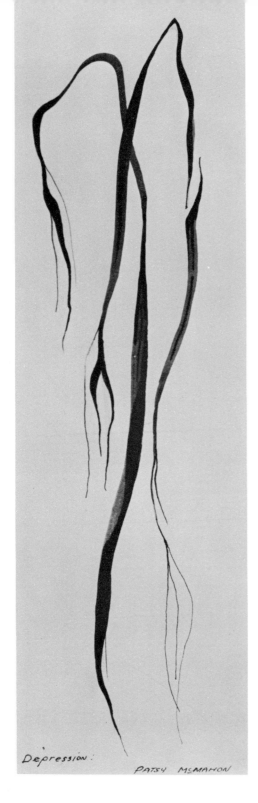

Depression:

PATSY McMAHON

Fig. 3-46. A free-brush and ink line expresses "depression."

Fig. 3-47. Tire tracks in the snow make an interesting line pattern of ridges. (Photograph courtesy of Goodyear Tire and Rubber Company.)

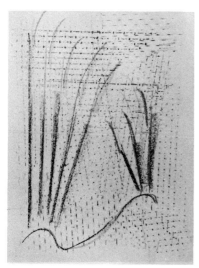

Fig. 3-48. Crayon lines over a textured background.

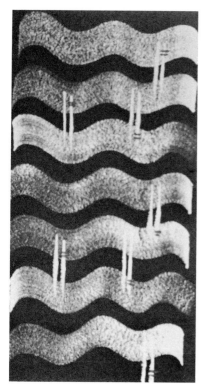

Fig. 3-49. A flat brush was pulled across the paper in a wavy manner to produce a soft line pattern.

cause of the dangling curves.

7. Art education students might like to imagine a story they could tell to a group of young children in experimenting with line. Have the children express with kinds and qualities of lines the incidents in the story.

Young Johnny started home from school. Many things interested him along the way. He skipped merrily along until he came to a field of daisies. He stopped to wander among them and pick a bouquet. A bee buzzed among them. He darted from the bee. Then he leisurely wandered over to a brook. He stood along the bank throwing pebbles into the water and watching the rings spread out. Tiring of that, he slipped over to Mr. Robinson's pasture; but the bull spied him and lumbered towards him. Johnny ran as fast as his feet would carry him and crawled under the fence. He ran towards home, panting and all out of breath. Finally he sat down on the side of the road to rest a while. In the shade of the trees and on this beautiful sunny day, he fell asleep.

With each of the line experiments strive for new arrangements that are carefully planned but which give a quality of casual freedom. Imagine that the design is for an all-over pattern for a place-mat, for wallpaper, for a formica cabinet top, a shopping bag, gift-wrapping paper, or whatever idea may appeal to the imagination. Develop an appreciation of the element of line for *itself* rather than expecting it to be used to represent something with which you are already familiar, such as a flower or an animal. In the latter case, you think more of the *shape* you are producing than the kind or quality of *line*.

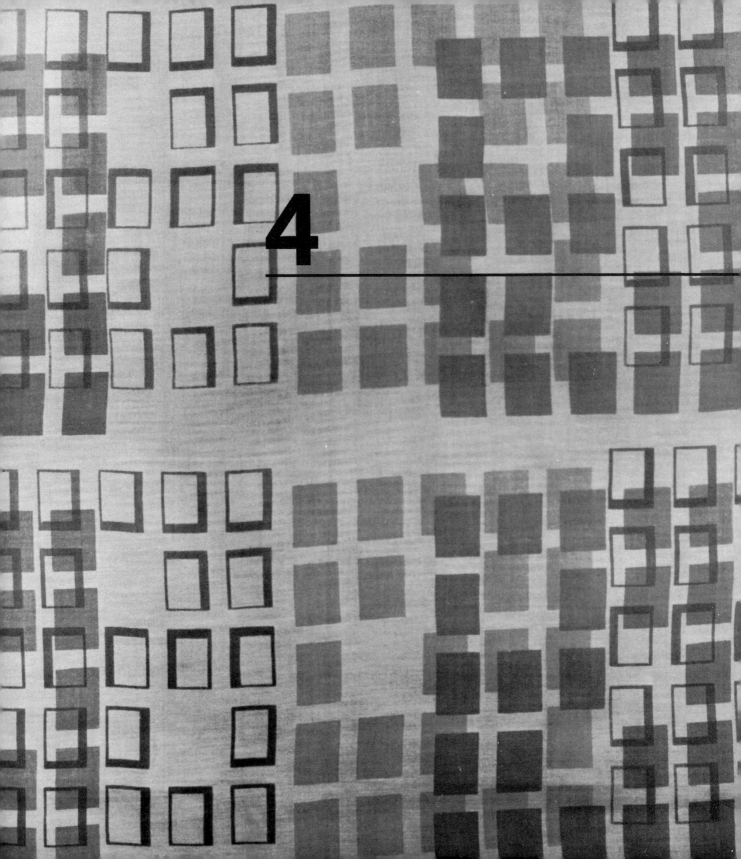

4

THE SHAPE OF THINGS

Extend a line around an area and what do you have?—a two-dimensional shape. Give this shape sides and a top and it becomes a three-dimensional form. In other words, *shape* may be viewed as a flat enclosure of space; *form* as volume surrounded by limiting factors.

We may be concerned with designing either a structural shape or a decorative one. The structural shape or form is that which is made by the length, width, depth, color, and texture of an area. It may be an actual shape, like a piece of paper, or a drawing of a shape on paper, or a three-dimensional model. A decorative shape is one which is used as surface enrichment of the structural design. In designing the structural shape or form we are concerned mainly with the following problems:

1. Is it beautifully proportioned?
2. Is it suited to its purpose?
3. Is it suited to the materials and processes which will be followed in making it?
4. Does it express individuality and creative thinking?

In creating the decorative design we are concerned with those same problems plus the following additional ones:

1. Does the decoration strengthen the shape of the object by emphasizing or harmonizing with its proportions?
2. Is the decoration used in moderation?

71

Fig. 4-1. The shapes of the stainless steel flatware express a quality of satisfactory structural design. They have character and beauty because of their fitness to their purpose. They have a frank simplicity of form, beautiful proportions, and the stainless steel is a material suited to both the purpose and the manufacturing process. (Variation #V, courtesy of Dansk Designs, Inc., Great Neck, New York.)

Fig. 4-2. The structural shape of the stainless steel flatware is simple and beautiful in proportion, as well as functional. However, to satisfy some individual tastes, a decorative design which is simple and is subordinated to the shape, actually adding strength to the structural form, has been added. (Variation #VI, courtesy of Dansk Designs, Inc., Great Neck, New York.)

Fig. 4-3. The very delicate long stem of the handblown cocktail glass of Lobmeyr crystal is a structural shape that would grace the most formal table. "Ambassador" pattern, Lobmeyr crystal. (Photograph courtesy of J. and L. Lobmeyr, Vienna, Austria. Designed by Professor Oswald Haerdtl of the Vienna Academy for Applied Arts, 1934.)

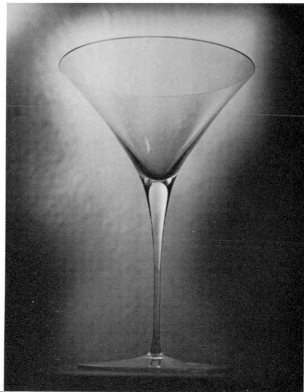

Fig. 4-4. The short-stemmed sherbet of the Royal Leerdam crystal has a sturdy, informal appearance. "Tango" pattern in Royal Leerdam. (Photograph courtesy of A. J. Van Dugteren and Sons, Inc.)

Fig. 4-5. The structural shapes of the flat abstract figures are simplified, exaggerated, and arranged in a playful, dancing manner. Each is a different shape, yet harmonizing with each other. For a Halloween centerpiece they would be a definite conversation piece.

(lower left)
Fig. 4-6. The design of the beautiful wooden candle holders fulfills all the requirements of a satisfactory structural design.

(lower right)
Fig. 4-7. The decorative design of hand inlaid polka dots on the neck and back of the amusing little giraffe fulfills the requirements of a satisfactory decorative design. (Photograph courtesy of Zoo-Line, Inc.)

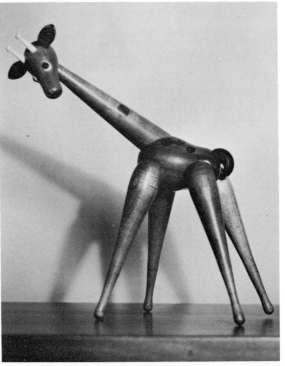

In this textbook we are mainly concerned with suggestions for creating designs for decorative purposes. However, in most chapters, the emphasis is on certain factors that are to be considered in the appreciation of good structural shapes. A student may apply his knowledge of a beautifully curved line to a design for a silk screen print, the curve of a clay pot in a a ceramics class, or the graceful shape of a chair back in a course in furniture design. It goes without saying that general principles of good design can be adapted for all areas of artistic expression.

Many terms may be used to classify shapes and forms, such as:

1. Representational, realistic, or natural
2. Abstract
3. Nonobjective
   a. Geometric
   b. Biomorphic or irregular

R E P R E S E N T A T I O N A L

We have often heard or read the old cliché that there is no place in art today for the artist who represents objects in a realistic manner because the camera can do his work so much better. We have also become familiar with the repeated criticism of nonobjective art: "My five-year old son could do as well." As a rebuttal to those ideas, let us think for a bit about the many areas of art in which precise accuracy in representation of a shape is most necessary—even today! What architect strives to show his sketches of his buildings in any except their true form? What industrial designer will find it to his advantage to abstract a shape? He may be employed to improve a product by changing its proportions or its mechanics of operation, but the sketches or the models which he makes are as near the final proportions of the actual product as he is capable of making them. In some commercial catalogs, it may not be practical to use photographs, so the artist makes renderings to represent actual objects advertised in the catalogs, which he portrays in a very realistic manner. The artist might portray specific details or eliminate others so much more efficiently than a camera would do in a similar job.

Fig. 4-8. In our study of the many ways one may use to create original designs, we must not overlook the beauty of natural forms. They may be admired for their own beauty, or for their inspiration to our imaginations.

Fig. 4-9. The rendering of a proposed building which an architect plans for a client must be sufficiently accurate in detail for the client to be able to visualize the actual building of the future. But the architect also depicts the shrubbery, trees, and people in a simple, abstract manner to add decorative touches to his rendering. (Architect's rendering of the Branch Facilities of the First Federal Savings and Loan Association, Lubbock, Texas. Schmidt and Stuart, A.I.A., Architects and Engineers.)

Most professional artists who work in an abstract or nonobjective manner have been trained in naturalistic representation in early classes in free-hand drawing. When they are thoroughly aware of every detail of the realistic form, *then* they can let their imaginations soar to higher levels of creative thinking. That road may lead them in paths of childlike simplicity of shape, as in the paintings by Miro, see Fig. 4-12, or to a more complicated form of abstraction as in Picasso's "Three Musicians." (See Fig. 4-13.) Whatever the final design may be, if it is a true work of art, it represents a varied background of training from realistic to nonobjective representation.

What we so often refer to as representational shapes are those which represent flowers, birds, fish, landscapes, etc., in an easily recognizable form. The petals on the rose curl back and show the drops of dew; the texture appears as soft velvet. Most realistic designs have little merit for *decorative* purposes. Most persons could recognize the confusion that would result in placing meat and potatoes on a flower-bedecked plate. A feeling of uneasy comfort may result from walking on a floral designed carpet. A scenic wallpaper seldom has more than passing appeal. A realistic sculpture of a noted person will often find its way into a dusty corner of a public building because of its mediocrity.

A true work of art needs more than an exact likeness to something from nature for it to have lasting appeal. It is quite possible the artist can give the design more character by introducing an unusual color combination or use a rendering technique that arouses the curiosity of passers-by. This, of course, is like portraying the "Boy with Green Hair" which immediately takes it out of the realm of the truly realistic. But as far as the element of shape is concerned, it could be as near the natural form as the artist could portray. He uses other elements, such as color and texture, to give it surprise and lasting beauty.

In Fig. 4-8 the natural form of the mesquite root may be admired from all angles for its beauty of proportion and variation of texture. It inspires the imagination to see any number of different associations. To one it might resemble a floppy eared dog. To another the element of form might be admired for itself because it does not suggest anything from nature except a beautiful form with pleasing proportions. To still another, it has no meaning at all except that it is "just an old mesquite root." In Fig. 4-9

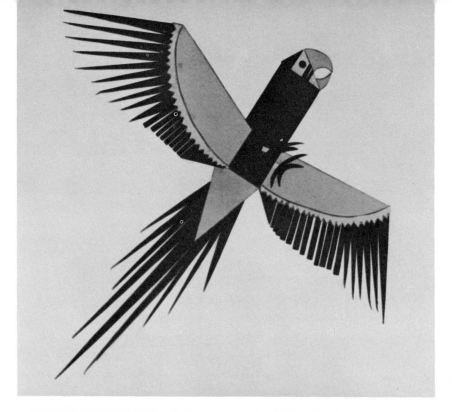

Fig. 4-10. An abstract bird design using a complicated arrangement of geometric shapes organized in a pleasing manner because of the harmony of shapes and gradation of size.

Fig. 4-11. An abstract animal design using a complicated arrangement of geometric shapes *not* organized in a pleasing manner because of the lack of harmony and the distorted placement of the shapes.

the architect's rendering of the building is done in a relatively realistic manner, whereas the people and trees and shrubbery are abstract.

ABSTRACT

The *abstract* shape may draw its inspiration from nature, but it is definitely man-created. He has modified and organized the subject matter to make it suit the purpose for which he is going to use the design. He makes it express certain qualities such as dignity, gaiety, or grotesqueness. He may *simplify, exaggerate, rearrange,* and in general make a planned organization that involves the expression of his imagination. It may be a flat design, or it may express depth. In the majority of instances when a design is to be enjoyed for pure pleasure, the abstract shape will "live" longer in our hearts. It may be a design on our china or crystal, a piece of sculpture, a painting, a dress fabric. If it is planned for lasting satisfaction, it will show a certain degree of abstraction. The simplification makes the design more easily understood or serves as a shorthand method of representation or symbolization. The *exaggeration* gives it more individuality. The *rearranging* brings the resulting attribute of harmony and fitness to purpose, tools, materials, and processes that will be followed in the completion of the design.

For emotional effects, a shape may be changed from its usual proportions to those that are more exaggerated or distorted. The early cross was designed with the horizontal bar about one-third the length of the vertical part. For deeper pull on the emotional heartstrings, look earnestly at the cross whose horizontal bar is about one-fifth the length of the vertical part. It draws the eyes upward and holds them in reverence as the designer had anticipated that it would.

The Oriental artist has long been noted for his ability to distort or exaggerate a part of a figure for the purpose of making it seem more important, whereas the less important was minimized by making it smaller than the usual proportions.

Any variation from the naturalistic shape is one which requires first, the use of the imagination to visualize, and second, the ability to execute the vision into a satisfactory abstract form. Nature provides a wide variety of shapes for us to see and enjoy, but these are only a few compared to the limitless variety that would be possible for the human mind to create

Fig. 4-12. *Composition, 1933,* by Joan Miro expresses a childlike simplicity of shape. (Gift of the Advisory Committee (by exchange). Collection The Museum of Modern Art.)

Fig. 4-13. *Three Musicians, 1921,* by Pablo Picasso expresses a more complicated form of abstraction. (Collection The Museum of Modern Art.)

(upper left)
Fig. 4-14. Triangles of various sizes and shapes are grouped together to suggest tall, stately "trees."

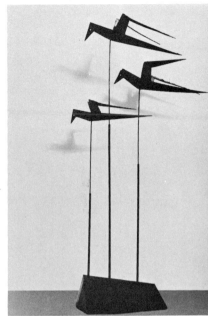

(upper right)
Fig. 4-15. Metal sculpture representing abstract bird forms constructed of basically geometric shapes. "Leaving the Nest," designed by Bill Lockhart.

(lower left)
Fig. 4-16. A group of abstract dancing figures show imaginative thinking in the use of the basically geometric shapes.

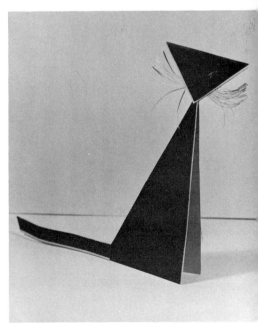

(lower right)
Fig. 4-17. Geometrically shaped pieces of cardboard fit together to create an amusing abstract "cat."

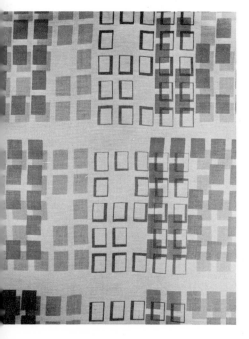

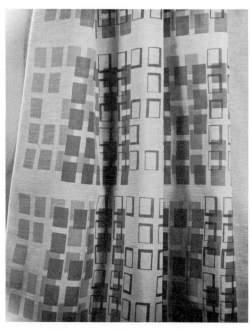

(upper left)
Fig. 4-18. Solid and linear rectangles, arranged in an overlapping pattern for an all-over repeat. "Geometrics," designed by Ethel Jane Beitler.

(upper right)
Fig. 4-19. For an all-over fabric design which will hang in folds, the design must not only look well flat, but enhanced by overlapping folds. "Geometrics," designed by Ethel Jane Beitler.

(lower left)
Fig. 4-20. Simple equilateral triangles may form hexagons and diamonds when combined in an all-over pattern. The irregularity of dark and light triangles lends added beauty to the pattern when it hangs in folds. "Triangles," designed by Alexander Girard for the Herman Miller Furniture Company.

(lower right)
Fig. 4-21. Large triangles and small squares form an interesting background pattern for the simple Christmas card design.

(upper left)
Fig. 4-22. Irregular shapes may be made more interesting sometimes by cutting into the side or making an open or hollow shape.

(upper right)
Fig. 4-23. Shadow patterns, or oil on water sometimes suggest a pattern of irregular shapes such as this one.

(lower left)
Fig. 4-24. Similar irregular shapes combine more successfully than do those which contrast more severely.

(lower right)
Fig. 4-25. The linear shapes are similar to the solid shapes and thus give sufficient contrast without being extreme.

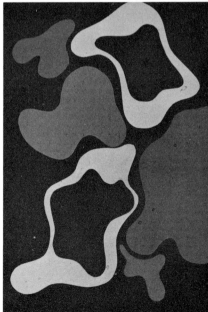

m its own imagination. The more we use the imagination, the more active it becomes. The more we resort to copying the ideas of others, the more difficult it becomes to use our own imaginations.

NONOBJECTIVE

A. GEOMETRIC SHAPES

A shape that we do not associate with anything from nature, such as saying it resembles a bird, a flower, etc., may be a mathematically precise shape such as a square, rectangle, triangle, circle, parallelogram, cube, or cylinder. These shapes are often thought of as having a dynamic or rigid quality. This beauty is derived either from this rhythmical ratio of proportions or their arrangement in relation to other shapes in a composition. Alexander Girard, in his fabric designs, has used simple geometric shapes of the most common type—squares and circles—and yet his spacing, his colors and variations in dark and light lend a note of excitement and interesting variety to each new design.

Geometric shapes such as squares, rectangles, and triangles have one quality in common, that of stability, because of their flat bases. Circles, ovals, spheres, and ellipses, however, have no true bases and seem to be, on the one hand, unstable and more capable of movement and, on the other hand, to possess a "built-in" quality of equilibrium.

In planning a geometric design there is sometimes the temptation to space the shapes in a very regular manner, mechanically measured and very regimental in character. The student of design must learn to develop a "feeling" for subtle irregularities of spacing, sizes of shapes, variation of dark and light and color. Instead of expecting that each design must be made according to set rules, his designs will acquire the delightful unexpectedness which makes art what it is.

The fabric design in Fig. 4-18 has made use of solid and linear rectangles arranged in an overlapping pattern for an all-over repeat. The overlapping gives the pattern depth. Common shapes like the equilateral triangle may be organized in an uncommon manner with pleasing irregularity of dark and light. (See Fig. 4-20.)

84

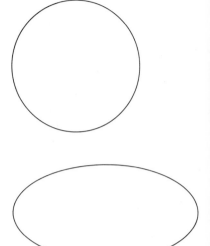

Fig. 4-26. Flat two-dimensional shapes.

Fig. 4-27. Flat two-dimensional shapes become "forms" when shading is added.

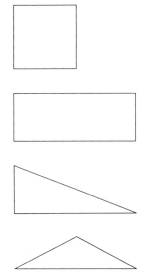

Fig. 4-28. Flat two-dimensional shapes with straight sides.

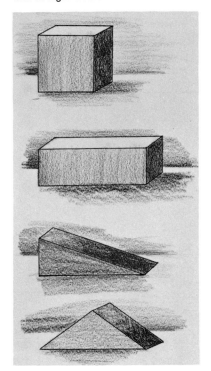

Fig. 4-29. When other sides are added, the "shapes" become "forms" and three-dimensional.

B. BIOMORPHIC OR IRREGULAR SHAPES

Frequently we may start out with a basically geometric shape and gradually change it to a free, irregular one. We may round the corners of a square, or dip in the sides in an irregular manner, making it a less precise but more intriguing shape. We may go further and open the shape in the center or cut into the side in an irregular manner. These shapes suggest to us the biomorphic shapes so frequently found in nature. The bean is basically a triangle with rounded corners. The apple is a circle with a dimple!

In Fig 4-22 compare the three irregular shapes. The first one has been made from a shape which was basically a triangle, but the angles were rounded and the sides curved inward. This takes away from the precise angularity and the measured accuracy of the triangle. In the second shape a few deeply curved notches have been cut into the long side, but note that these notches, for more pleasing proportions, vary in size and are not cut right in the center of the side. In the third shape the center has been cut away in an irregular manner, making the sides of the broad angle relatively thick, whereas the long side is thin and has a break in it off-center.

In Fig. 4-23 a variety of irregular shapes harmonize with each other and fit together almost like a jig-saw puzzle. In Fig. 4-30 similar irregular shapes are organized for a serigraph. They seem to have been suggested by a pattern of cut slabs of stone.

The fact that shapes are related not only make them harmonize with each other more satisfactorily for a design, but it may also give the design added meaning and character. Compare the shapes in Figs. 4-31 and 32. The shapes in Fig. 4-31 express softness because of the graceful curves, whereas the shapes in Fig. 4-32 express harshness because of the sharp angles.

DEFINITION OF "FORM"

Thus far in this chapter we have referred almost entirely to the element of shape. It might be well at this point to differentiate between our meaning of the terms shape and form. We may draw a circle which we refer to as a "shape." It is flat and two-dimensional in character. But when we add shading to express light and shadow, the "circle-shape" becomes a rounded "form" with substance and new meaning. It seems three-dimensional and gives the suggestion that it may be viewed from all angles.

In Fig. 4-27 the flat two-dimensional shapes shown in Fig. 4-26 have had shading added so they appear as round and oval spherical forms which have a three-dimensional character. In Fig. 4-29 the flat two-dimensional shapes shown in Fig. 4-28 have had other sides added besides the shading so they also become "forms" and three-dimensional.

FUNCTION OF SHAPE AND FORM

Let us assume we are designing a rectangular shape to be used basically as a living-room. It might be made 15′ x 18′. Or if it is to be used for a combination living and dining area, 15′ x 21′ might be a better proportion. As far as pleasing proportions are concerned, each shape might be equally satisfactory, but to suit the functions for which it will be used, the shape must be varied accordingly.

If a design is to become a piece of tableware made from glass, one would wish to know whether it was to be used every day or for special occasions. Relatively heavy glass such as the "Tango" pattern in Royal Leerdam crystal is quite appropriate in a short-stemmed goblet for informal use. (See Fig. 4-4.) Delicate handblown glass, on the other hand, such as that in "Ambassador" pattern in Lobmeyr crystal becomes even more delicate when designed with a long stem for more formal use. (See Fig. 4-3.)

We cannot judge each shape or form and say that it is entirely lacking in beauty, because the purpose for which we are planning to use it will determine to a large extent the proper evaluation of it. It might be unsatisfactory for one purpose, but be very fine for another use. One's tastes will naturally enter into our evaluation of a "good shape" for a particular function. If we can learn to look at a design in a broadminded manner and apply the principles of design, the resulting organization of the elements will no doubt be a happy solution of the problem. We will need to make many trial arrangements of the elements in order to choose finally the most satisfactory one. This is by no means a waste of time, however,

Fig. 4-30. Irregular shapes which might have been suggested by a pattern of cut slabs of stone. Serigraph, "Fossilforms," by Dean Meeker. (Photograph courtesy of Quepha Rawls, owner.)

Fig. 4-31. Related irregular shapes which express softness because of the graceful curves.

Fig. 4-32. Related irregular shapes which express harshness because of the sharp angles.

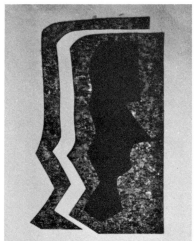

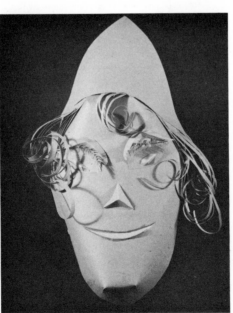

(upper left)
Fig. 4-33. A basic triangular shape may suggest an abstract mask.

(upper right)
Fig. 4-34. Circles scored on opposite sides give three-dimensional effects for eyes and nose. The exaggeration of size of the eyes, nose, and mouth also give a different personality to the mask.

(lower left)
Fig. 4-35. Curls of paper add interest for beards, hair, and lashes.

(lower right)
Fig. 4-36. Amusing, sad, or droll personalities can easily be expressed by experimenting with paper shapes.

Fig. 4-37. Similar irregular shapes become more interesting with overlapping and contrast of dark and light.

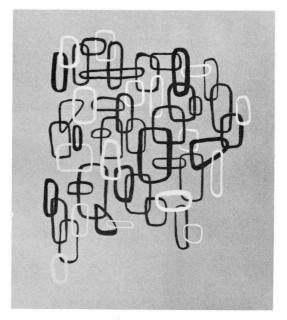

Fig. 4-38. One basic shape cut in an irregular manner and fit together to create two related shapes.

Fig. 4-39. Simple abstract shapes related by movement and direction.

Fig. 4-40. Basically geometric shapes adapted in a three-dimensional manner.

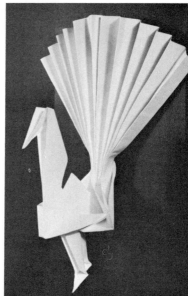

A

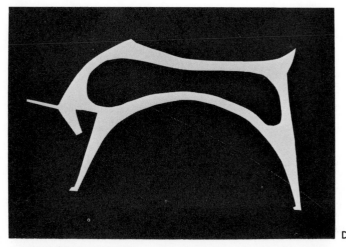

D

Fig. 4-41. With imagination and scraps of paper, exciting abstract birds, animals, fish, and human figure designs take shape.

B

E

C

for by this method we develop skill, a better sense of discrimination, and may eventually arrive at a technique of working which may be characterized as distinctly our own. This is what most artists are striving for.

Lines within the material, such as the grain in wood, may suggest to the artist the form of the object which can be made from it. The curve of a grain line may suggest the upward swing of an arm for the sculpture of a figure. The series of irregular curves may remind him of the folds of drapery in a skirt. If we are constantly aware of the many characteristics in materials we shall find that we will continually design with them in mind. We will not force the material to do what it does not wish to do. We will let it work for us and with us.

The tools and processes or techniques used in making an object will definitely alter its form. In making a piece of wood sculpture, if one has only a knife to whittle with, the size of the form may be small. If one has a power saw, he may use a large piece of wood and take off large areas of wood which he does not want for the final design. These pieces, in turn, may give inspiration for other designs which can be made from them. But if one has only carving tools, the extra wood must be cut off in small gouges, thus becoming wood shavings which may or may not be usable for other designs.

CREATIVE EXPERIMENTS

1. To develop an awareness of interesting shapes and forms:
    a. Find examples of beautifully proportioned shapes and forms in nature: pebbles, leaves, driftwood, and any other natural forms.
    b. Find illustrations of beautiful natural shapes and forms: pictures of trees, flowers, animals, birds, fish.
    c. Find examples of exciting new shapes in actual objects or illustrations of man-made functional designs: a molded plastic or plywood chair, an automobile fin, a piece of tableware, a new collar shape, a beautiful bottle (other shapes too numerous to list). Only the imagination and one's sensitivity to pleasing proportions would be the limiting factors in one's ability to find these examples.
    d. Find illustrations or actual examples of abstract and nonobjective shapes and forms in fabrics, wallpaper, sculpture, paintings.

2. To experiment with creating shapes and forms:

   a. Use cut paper or draw several rectangles of varying sizes and shapes to compare their proportions.

   b. Use cut paper or draw several shapes appropriate for silhouettes of vases, tumblers, goblets, or other tableware.

   c. Use one of your line designs and interpret it in terms of shape.

   d. Cut several geometric shapes of varying sizes. Make irregular shapes out of them by rounding an occasional corner or dipping in the side.

   e. If the student has saved all of his scraps of paper from the above designs, these may suggest other abstract designs which could be assembled to represent amusing birds, animals, fish, or human figures.

   f. Plan an all-over pattern of repeated shapes for wallpaper or gift-wrapping paper.

   g. Plan a three-dimensional form which could be carved from wood or soap.

   h. Find a piece of scrap wood which is a beautiful form and finish it for a piece of nonobjective sculpture.

5

SPACE—ALL OR NOTHING

Space is *nothing* until a point of reference is established. To establish this point of reference, we need to enclose or limit the space surrounding this point of reference. One may plan a certain size enclosure, or the limitations may be the edge of the canvas on which an artist is painting, or the walls of the room which one is furnishing, or the whole out-of-doors as far as one can see. Space is *all of the area* within the enclosure or the outer fringe of our vision.

Spatial organization is three-dimensional in character because it is the correlation of a whole area. Spatial organization includes the design of the shapes, the textures, and the colors within the space in relation to the whole space. If one were planning the furnishings for a room, there would be many ways in which one could study the total space. Such ways would consist of the following:

1. The floor space and the relative amount of area that each piece of furniture would occupy.

2. Each wall space with its relative amount of area that various pieces of furniture and accessories occupy when placed against the wall, plus any architectural features, such as windows and doors.

3. The ceiling space with its division, and with beams or lighting fixtures.

4. The smaller areas of space in open shelves and on table and desk tops.

95

Most of our cities today are examples of myriads of buildings, huddled together with very little planning of the whole spatial organization. The plans of the city remodelers of today call for expensive demolishing of buildings, clearing large areas for super-highways, shopping centers, parking areas, and housing projects. If the designers of the past could have foreseen the future and could have had the cooperation of the citizens in planning their "City of the Future," the space could have been organized in a much more beautiful and efficient manner, so that today we could go on and merely add to the building of the city without first tearing down the old.

TWO-DIMENSIONAL SPACE

Before one can thoroughly understand all the underlying principles with which one would be concerned in the total spatial organization, one must first begin with a study of simple two-dimensional space. Let us enclose a definite size area as in Fig. 5-1A. This enclosure has length and width. Within this enclosure we may place another shape which is defined by an outline as in diagram B. Our eyes then become aware of the space surrounding the inner shape and also the space within that shape. As we add other shapes to the space, tensions are created, causing the eyes to move from one shape to another in the order of their importance. The closer together objects are grouped, the more conscious we are of the *shapes*. The further apart, the more conscious we are of *space*. Our decision to emphasize one element in preference to another might be due to the *utilitarian* or to the *esthetic* characteristics of the design, or both.

In diagrams C and D the movement in the space was created by means of contrast in the size and shapes. Movement might also be created by changing the directions of the shapes as in diagram E.

Contrast of values in the shapes helps to intensify the feeling of movement in space, as in diagram F.

The problems of placement of shapes in space involve all the principles of design, but more specifically the problem of proportion. In Chapter 2 in the discussion of this principle we made reference to the various ways in which space might be divided, employing repetition, variety, and a

96

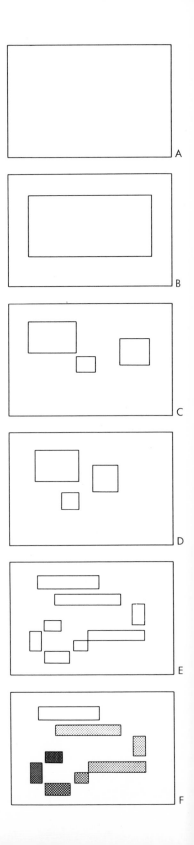

Fig. 5-1. Diagrams of movement in two-dimensional space.

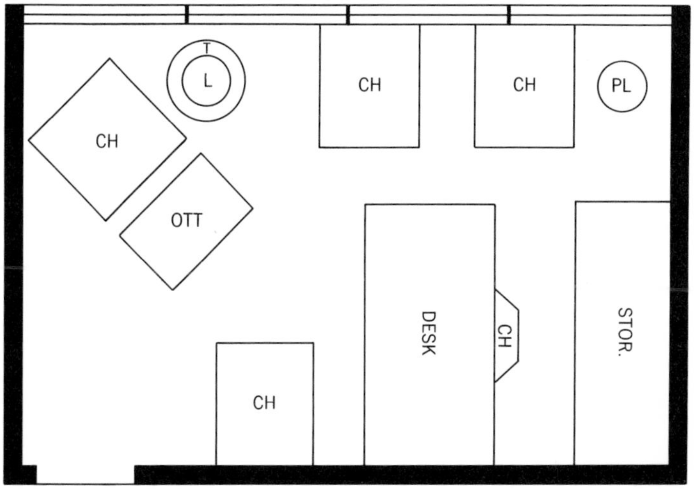

Fig. 5-2. The room is so crowded with furniture there is not sufficient room to move about comfortably.

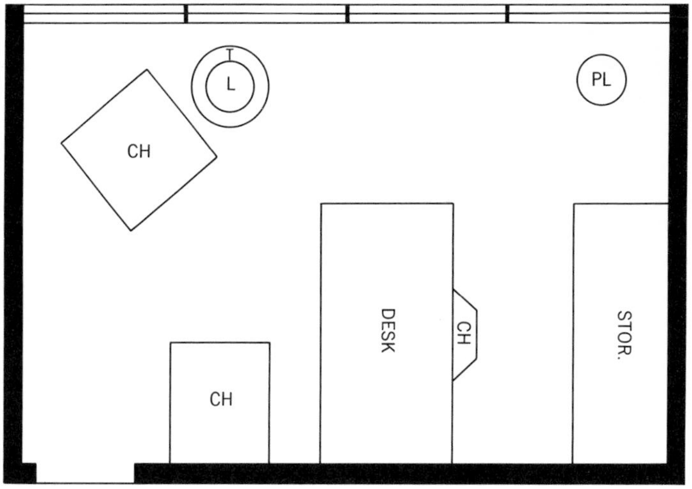

Fig. 5-3. By reducing the number of pieces of furniture, the room actually appears larger and is also much more convenient in arrangement.

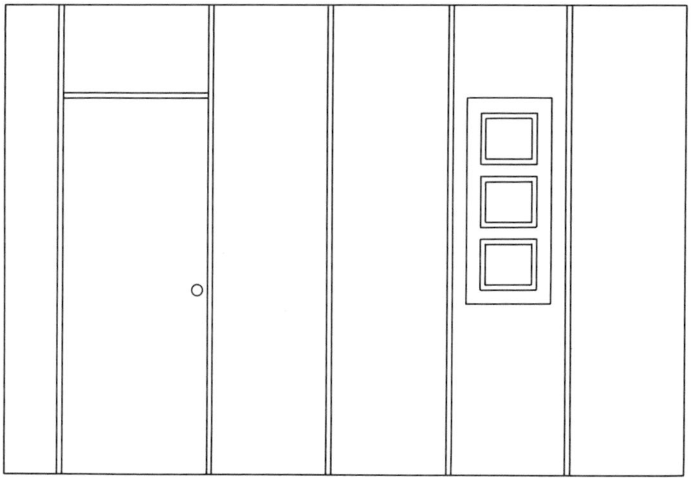

Fig. 5-4. The vertical divisions serve two purposes: (1) they might make the ceiling appear higher or (2) the length of the wall space might be made to appear shorter because the space is broken.

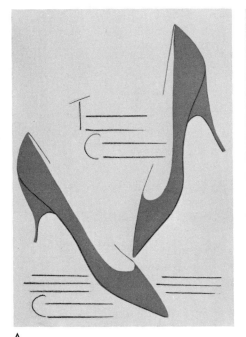

A

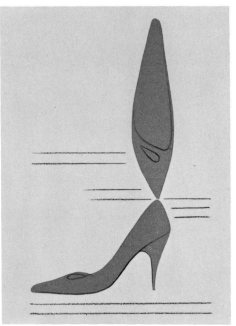

B

Fig. 5-5. Experiments with thumbnail sketches of layouts help one in arriving at a satisfactory arrangement of space.

C

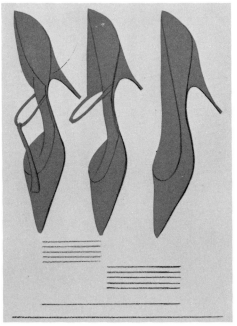

D

combination of repetition and variety. We suggest that the reader refer back to those paragraphs.

For purposes of helping the reader to become aware of the many ways in which the information in these chapters can be applied to various areas of life, let us apply to a room our discussion of the division of space. First, we must plan the floor space and locate the various pieces of furniture to scale. Correct planning of this kind will aid one in selecting the right scale of furniture and the correct number of pieces to fit the available space. A salesman might do a successful job of selling to a client a large desk, desk chair, credenza, lounge chair, and several guest chairs for his office. When his client has them delivered, however, he finds there is not room for all of them. If some preplanning had been done on paper first, the salesperson could have advised the client to select a smaller desk, credenza, and lounge chair. Or he could have left out the credenza and kept the large lounge chair. The diagram would also have indicated the amount of space available between the various pieces of furniture to allow for utilitarian as well as esthetic needs. See Figs. 5-2, 5-3.

A diagram of a wall area will allow the client to visualize architectural and decorative features which would need to be considered in relation to the furnishings. A high ceiling or a long wall space might be broken by strips of walnut to add color and distinction to the room. The diagram will also show the division of space. See Fig. 5-4.

The "open-stock" storage walls that are being produced today by a number of different manufacturing firms provide a challenge in selecting and organizing open and closed shelf space, drawer and filing space, provision for television, dictaphone, record player, and other equipment as the individual so desires. Most of the storage components are suspended from the wall or from metal poles that span the space from floor to ceiling. The problem is one of breaking up the wall space in a pleasing and usable manner. Turn back to page 3, Fig. 1-1, to see the example of the Herman Miller Comprehensive Storage System as displayed in a show room as it might be organized for an office space or a home.

A commercial artist plans his division of space for a layout of an advertisement so that he can decide what area is going to have copy, what part will be devoted to illustration, and where the firm name will be placed. A number of quick thumbnail sketches will give him a variety of ideas for his space organization. See Figs. 5-5A, B, C, and D.

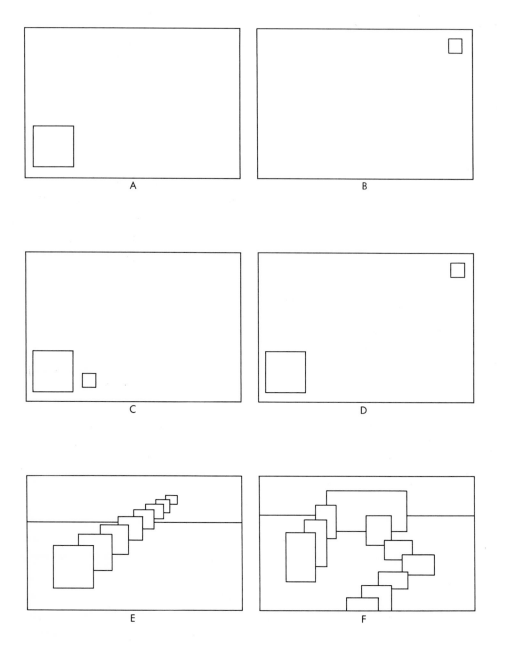

Fig. 5-6. Size and placement of objects within an enclosure suggest varying degrees of distance or movement in space.

A

B

C

D

E

F

THREE-DIMENSIONAL SPACE

The addition of a third dimension, that of depth, may be evidenced in the placement of shapes within a space. Contrast of size added to the placement intensifies the illusion of depth. In Fig. 5-6A, note that the shape appears to be in the foreground because it is relatively large and placed at the bottom of the space. In B the shape appears to be in the background, or far away, because it is relatively small and placed at the top of the space.

In diagram C the base of the shapes is on the same level, so that they appear to vary a great deal in size. In diagram D the optical illusion is created of depth, and the actual shapes could be the same size if the small ones were moved closer to the front.

In diagram E the feeling of distance is created by the gradual decrease in size of the square as it moves into the background, whereas in F the shapes not only move into the background but come back into the foreground again.

We may create the illusion of volume by means of the placement of planes in space, or we may keep the space open and "untrapped." In Fig. 5-7 the planes touch only at the base, but they seem to enclose the space; whereas in Fig. 5-8 the planes touch and bisect, but the space is not trapped or enclosed. In some fields of architecture the walls seem to enclose space in a compact way, whereas in others the glass walls cause the interior and exterior walls to blend together and suggest open space.

Architects, painters, and commercial artists must have a thorough understanding of the ways of representing three-dimensional space by means of perspective. Earlier in this chapter we discussed the advisability of preplanning the furnishings of a room. More detailed rendering of the furnishings and architectural features could be shown by applying simple rules of perspective.

Very frequently painters and commercial artists alter true perspective for the sake of emphasis. Painters will sometimes purposely indicate several sets of vanishing points within one picture in order to give a feeling of movement. Instead of presenting one static view to the viewer, the impression is given that the objects seen in the picture are being viewed from several vantage points.

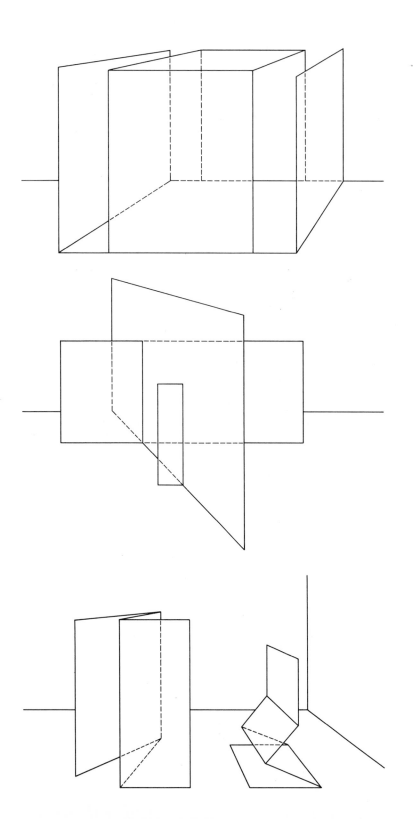

Fig. 5-7. Close to the vertical end pieces open areas have been left; thus the entire construction is an example of partially enclosed space.

Fig. 5-8. The planes placed at right angles do not enclose any area of space at any point.

Fig. 5-9. The spaces become smaller and more "enclosed" as we approach the folds, or as the angles between the folds become sharper.

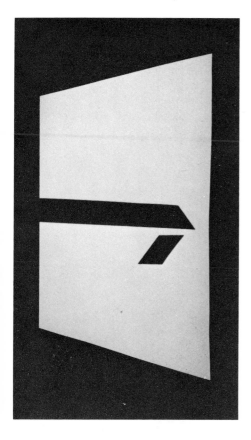 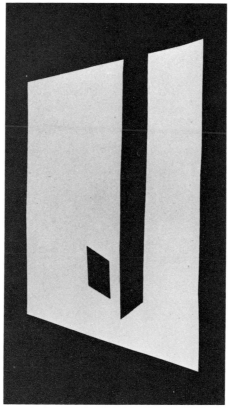 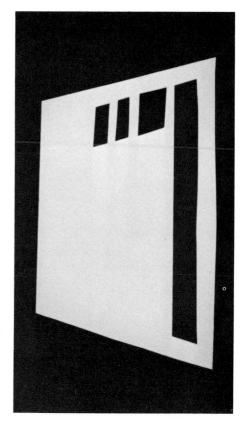

Fig. 5-10A. The horizontal line creates the optical illusion of widening the space in the enclosure.

Fig. 5-10B. The vertical line creates the optical illusion of making the space in the enclosure appear taller.

Fig. 5-10C. Both vertical and horizontal movement create the optical illusion of making the space appear wider and taller.

Fig. 5-11. Decrease in size of shapes plus raising the value of dark and light in the shadows creates a strong effect of distance.

Fig. 5-12A. The values of dark and light in the angles and sweeping curve are all the same, thus creating no strong feeling of distance except that which is felt by the gradation of size.

Fig. 5-12B. The gradation of values in the angular shapes as well as gradation of size produces a stronger feeling of distance.

A

B

CREATIVE EXPERIMENTS

1. To develop an awareness of space and ways that it can be expressed:

   a. Make a list of as many words as you can which would describe different kinds of space—actual, relative, inner, outer, surface, imaginative, aerial, infinite, hollow, two-dimensional, three-dimensional, moving, etc.

   b. Find examples in magazines that would illustrate some of the above words or others on your list.

   c. Find examples in magazines of:

   (1) A "bird's-eye" view of space, as though you were in an airplane looking down on an area.

   (2) A scene in which the objects in the foreground were bright and clear in color and those in the background were hazy, showing more distance.

   (3) An artist's sketch using perspective to show distance from a vanishing point.

   d. Find examples of optical illusions which express impressions of space.

2. To experiment with creating examples of space and space division:

   a. Draw four rectangles which you consider are pleasing in proportion for enclosing space.

   b. Use all straight lines and divide the above rectangles into horizontal areas expressing:

   (1) gradation of size

   (2) repetition

   (3) variation

   (4) repetition and variation

   c. In a vertical rectangle, use shapes to express movement and distance (or a third-dimension).

   d. Make several tracings of (c) and experiment with dark and light values, and color to create different effects of distance.

   e. Use pieces of cardboard or balsa wood to experiment with examples of partially enclosed and open space, using at least three planes in each construction.

   f. Make a three-dimensional construction to be hung from the ceiling so it will move freely in space (a mobile).

6

COLOR SOUNDS OFF

With our galaxy of colors in our homes, offices, factories, stores, our garments, our vehicles of transportation, it is difficult to imagine a world without color. Yet how many people go through life unaware of the beauty of color? But it has been only a generation ago, approximately, that our automobiles were predominantly black, our walls were tan, garments were largely black or white, factory walls were whitewashed or made a dismal gray like the machines. In ancient times dyes and pigments were so precious they were used as currency, kings' ransoms, and royal gifts. Only a rich man could afford colored garments and the more they reeked of strong dyes, the greater was the sign of his wealth and importance.

In early Colonial days in America, housewives were noted for their particular formulas for certain dyes. When other housewives wanted their yarns dyed they would take some to "Mrs. Jones" to have them dyed brown, to "Mrs. Smith" for some to be dyed red, others to "Mrs. Bailey" to have them dyed yellow. The Colonial storekeeper had only a few bolts of fabric in only a small variety of colors. Today it is sometimes difficult to choose because of the many, many colors in all fabrics. As our knowledge and availability of color increase, so does our demand for an even greater variety of forms and colors in our fabrics, our paints, and our furnishings.

One may study color from any one of four scientific approaches.

1. The *physiologist* studies color from the way it is received by the eye. Factory employers have performed fatigue experiments to determine how they could get their employees to produce more work with greater ease by means of color conditioning their surroundings. Color safety codes in some cases cut the accident ratio as much as 45 per cent. Colored work areas are planned to reduce eye strain and fatigue, and rest areas are planned in colors for relaxation.

2. The psychologist studies how a person is affected emotionally by the colors he sees and how colors are affected by one another. The United States Navy has found that submarine crews have better health, morale, and efficiency in spite of their restricted space and long days under the surface when there is beautiful planning of the colors for the submarine interior.

We have become so familiar with judging the quality of food by its color that many sensitive individuals would not enjoy a dinner of purple steak, green butter, blue potatoes, red bread, and chartruese milk. One experiment has dealt with changing the basic color of foods. After eating bright green mashed potatoes, many people were unable to recognize this strange food, even though the taste had not been changed. Psychiatrists tell us that many of our divorces are the result of unsatisfactory color in surroundings. One husband may become irritable and morose if the walls are yellow and brown. A wife may be affected in a similar way by forms of red and blue. Most individuals have color likes and dislikes and are affected emotionally by those hues in their surroundings. Colors which appeal to children may seem garish to adults. Colors which appeal to the underprivileged and uneducated may be entirely different from those that the more cultured or wealthy would choose. This may also be true of nationalities of different temperate zones.

3. The *physicist* studies wavelengths and intensities of light. The experiments by physicists illustrate the fact that colored lights, when mixed, do not produce the same results as would be secured by mixing pigments of the same hues. The physicist is working with light rays, whereas pigments are colored matter of either mineral or vegetable origin. A colored surface absorbs or subtracts from white light and wavelengths of all the colors except its own, and so gives the impression of that particular color. Colored lights may be mixed to form any number of brilliant colors as

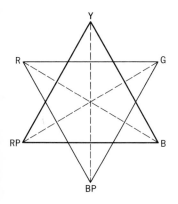

Fig. 6-1. The physicist develops his color theory around a six-hue wheel. In light, the blue-purple is complementary to the yellow, the blue is complementary to the red, and the red-purple is complementary to the green.

well as white. In the light theory red, green, and blue-purple are the three primaries instead of the red, blue, and yellow in the pigment theory. The three secondary colors, as they are seen in light, are yellow, red-purple, and blue. These secondaries are produced as follows: yellow light is secured by mixing red and green lights; red-purple results from mixing red and blue-purple; blue light is secured by mixing green and blue-purple. In Fig. 6-1, the dotted lines connect complementary pairs which will neutralize each other when combined and will produce white light. The lighting engineer for dramatic productions can create color effects with lights by the flick of a switch that would take the painter hours of labor and gallons of paint to achieve. Sometimes whole backgrounds can be entirely changed by the use of different lights. Certain chemicals, such as zinc, phospherine, and radium bromide, can also change the color effects when various lights are reflected on them. They might even change the appearance of a surface from a pattern to a solid color.

4. The *chemist* studies the chemical properties of the natural and artificial coloring materials used for the manufacture of dyes and paints. He knows that pigments mix differently and produce different hues from mixtures of colored lights. He experiments with definite formulas for mixing paints so one may be assured of always being able to match a particular color. He tests problems of fading, washing, cracking, peeling, and spreading consistencies. He seeks new sources of pigments and dyes.

A number of systems for the study of color has been devised. Two are in common use today: the Prang System and the Munsell System. To avoid confusion in the mind of the beginning student only the Prang theory will be discussed in detail. For further study and comparison of the two systems it is suggested that the reader use Munsell's *Color Atlas and Color Notation* and *A Practical Description of the Munsell Color System* by T. M. Cleland.

THE PRANG COLOR SYSTEM

We need some way of describing the general characteristics of color. For this reason the three ways in which colors may be said to differ are in their *hue, value,* and *intensity.* These terms are referred to synono-mously as *properties, qualities,* or *dimensions* of color.

1. *Hue*—the name of the color, such as red or blue-green.
2. *Value*—the lightness or darkness of the color.
3. *Intensity*—the brightness or dullness of the color.

All these dimensions may be used to describe every form of color, just as height, width, and depth may be used to describe an object.

HUE

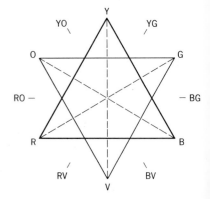

Fig. 6-2. Prang develops his color theory around a twelve-hue circle. The heavy line connects the primary hues; the fine line connects the secondary hues; and the intermediate hues are shown in between each of the primary and secondary hues.

Hues may be classified in a number of different ways.

Warm and cool hues. Those hues which have varying amounts of the red that we associate with fire are identified as warm, whereas those which have differing amounts of blue in them give more the effect of coolness. Colors which are on the borderline are yellow and violet. Yellow appears more warm because of its association with sunshine, and more cool because of its lightness in value. Violet is a mixture of both red and blue. Warm hues are more advancing and make objects appear larger, whereas cool ones are more receding and decrease apparent size. This could be used to advantage in an interior. If a room is small, cool hues might make it seem larger, whereas large areas of warm hues would only make it seem still smaller.

Arrangement on the Color Wheel. Hues may be classified as primary, secondary, or binary, and intermediate for purposes of organization on a color wheel. In Fig. 6-2 note that the heavy line connecting the primary hues of red, blue, and yellow form an equilateral triangle. These hues are the ones which are most important. No other hues can be mixed to obtain them. They are the basis for all other forms of color.

The finer line connecting the secondary hues of green, orange, and violet also form an equilateral triangle. The green is placed half-way between the yellow and blue because equal amounts of yellow and blue are mixed to make green. Equal amounts of blue and red are mixed to form violet, and also equal amounts of red and yellow form orange. Actually the equal mixing of two primary colors to form a secondary color works in theory. You will find many of the paints you purchase will not mix to form a true and accurate color.

Color Wheel

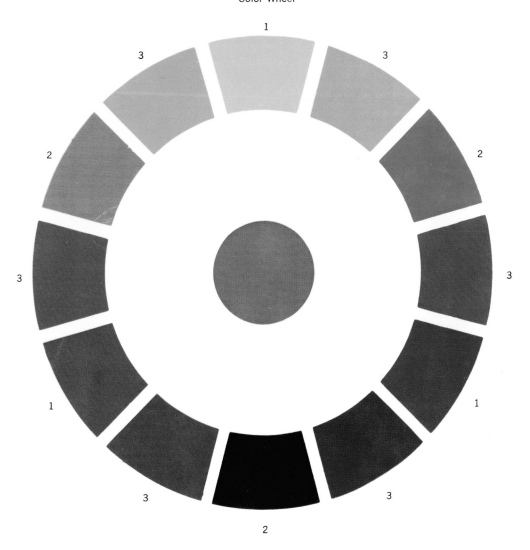

Fig. 6-3. The Prang color wheel is divided into three groups of hues. Those marked (1) are the Primary hues; those marked (2) are the Secondary hues; those marked (3) indicate the Intermediate hues. Reading clockwise around the circle, the colors are: yellow, yellow-green, green, blue-green, blue, blue-violet, violet, red-violet, red, red-orange, orange, and yellow-orange.

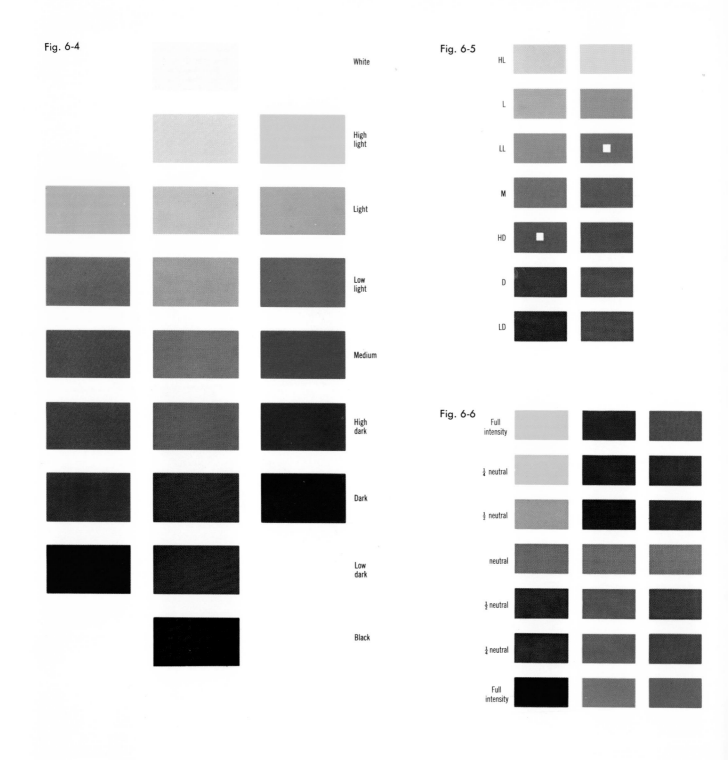

Fig. 6-4

White

High
light

Light

Low
light

Medium

High
dark

Dark

Low
dark

Black

Fig. 6-5

HL

L

LL

M

HD

D

LD

Fig. 6-6

Full
intensity

$\frac{1}{4}$ neutral

$\frac{1}{2}$ neutral

neutral

$\frac{1}{2}$ neutral

$\frac{1}{4}$ neutral

Full
intensity

(extreme left)
Fig. 6-4. Normal value scale. Standard value scale with the normal equivalents in hues shown in relation to the steps on the value scale.

(upper right)
Fig. 6-5. Value scale of red and orange. Each hue has a normal value (the one with the white square) and may be raised or lowered from the normal value.

(lower right)
Fig. 6-6. Intensity scale. Each hue may be changed in intensity by adding the complement until the neutral gray is reached.

Each intermediate hue has a compound name composed of the primary and secondary hues which are used to mix it. For instance, yellow-green is a mixture of the primary yellow and the secondary green. Blue-green is a mixture of the primary blue and the secondary green. You may produce each intermediate hue by the mixture of a primary and secondary hue and it is placed half-way between these hues. If you were to mix the primary and secondary hues (for instance, yellow and green) there would be any number of different proportions of the two that you might use, but the resulting hue would still be classified in this case as yellow-green. It might be identified as a yellow yellow-green, a yellow-green, or a green yellow-green. Munsell has a notation system which enables one to determine the approximate amount of yellow and green that is present in the yellow-green, but Prang has no set formula or system for identification of each variation of the intermediate hues.

Normal, Standard, and Popular Hues. A hue which is a pure pigment is known as a *normal* hue. For practical purposes Prang has indicated only twelve normal hues on his color circle, but it would be possible with the many variations of intermediate hues to recognize approximately one hundred different normal hues. A hue is changed into another hue by adding a neighboring primary or secondary hue to it. For example, yellow plus green equals yellow-green, or yellow plus blue equals green. Or a transparent film of a neighboring hue may be placed over the original hue to change the appearance of both hues.

The six normal hues which are most frequently used are classified as standard hues and are the ones usually found in a child's box of paints. They are red, yellow, blue, green, orange, and violet. In the pigment theory of color, black, gray, and white are not classified as hues but as neutrals. The *neutrals* will be discussed under the heading of "value." Many familiar names of colors do not appear on the color wheel. Pink, lavender, tan, brown, beige are names which are given to various values and intensities of colors. Most of these *popular* names of colors are coined by manufacturers for the purpose of advertising their merchandise each season. The various forms of colors take on new fashionable connotations and cause others to become "dated" and unpopular. For instance, one season the fashionable color might be "Evergreen," a dark value and moderately grayed form of green. Another season a similar type of green, except perhaps a bit darker in value, might be referred to as "Forest Green."

If one has a thorough understanding of the dimension of hue, he should be able to:

1. Describe the color as far as its proper name and location on the color wheel.
2. Recognize its advancing and receding properties.
3. Recognize its qualities of warmth and coolness.

VALUE

The second dimension of color is value, or the variation in darkness and lightness. If one were to add varying amounts of black to white one could recognize many different degrees of darkness and lightness. For practical purposes, however, we usually use only seven values of gray in between the white and the black. These are arranged in regular manner in a chart referred to as a *Value Scale*. (See chart in Fig. 6-4 and 6-5.) This scale shows the neutral in the center with the equivalent normal hues in relation to each value of gray. No color can be as light as white or as dark as black. If one were to draw a line between each pair of colors, as in Fig. 6-3, one could see how the hues, as they are arranged on the color wheel, fall automatically in the same arrangement as they are placed on the value scale. You will also note, therefore, that the normal hues show a natural variation in darkness and lightness. For instance, yellow is the lightest and is placed as the equivalent of the high-light in value. Yellow-green and yellow-orange are darker and are placed as the equivalent of light. Green and orange are still darker and are placed as the equivalent of low-light, and so on to violet which is the equivalent of low-dark.

You will also discover that the value of each normal hue may be changed by the addition of white or water to raise the value, or black to lower the value. Thus, a *tint* is any value above normal and a *shade* is any value below normal for that particular hue. For example, adding a small amount of white to violet would produce a tint of violet even though this tint would fall as the equivalent of dark or high-dark on the value scale. It is possible to raise the value of every hue to a value just under white,

114

Fig. 6-7

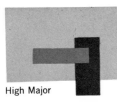

High Major

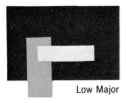

Low Major

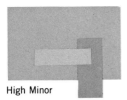

High Minor

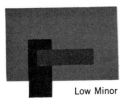

Low Minor

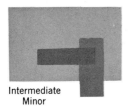

Intermediate
Minor

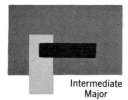

Intermediate
Major

and lower it to a value just above black. For practical purposes, a value of yellow above high-light and a value of violet below low-dark would not be included on the standard chart, but it would be possible to recognize those values with the eye.

Value Keys. In choosing the various values to be used together in a particular composition a series of value keys have been developed to aid the student in making reference to or describing a particular arrangement of values. These "keys" utilize the terms "major" and "minor" to signify strong contrast of values, or the same or similar values respectively. We mentioned earlier in this chapter that values above medium were referred to as "high values" and those below medium as "low values." Therefore, by combining these terms with the words "major" and "minor" we can arrive at the following "value keys." (See Fig. 6-7.)

1. *High minor key*—same or similar values with no more than three steps apart on the value scale, and all above medium in value. (They may be any hue or neutrals.)

2. *High major key*—strong contrast of dark and light values with at least five steps difference in values with a larger area of high value (above medium) than low. (They may be any hue, or neutrals.)

3. *Low minor key*—same or similar values with no more than three steps apart on the value scale, and all below medium in value. (They may be any hue or neutrals.)

4. *Low major key*—strong contrast of dark and light values with at least five steps difference in values with a larger area of low values (below medium) than high. (They may be any hue or neutrals.)

5. *Intermediate minor key*—same or similar values with no more than three steps apart on the value scale, and all in the middle part of the value scale. (They may be any hue or neutrals.)

6. *Intermediate major key*—strong contrast of dark and light values with at least five steps difference in values with a larger area of medium value. (They may be any hue or neutrals.)

Order of Values. The standard value scale with its equivalent normal hues becomes a very valuable chart to keep in mind when combining different forms of colors. There are those combinations in which the colors seem to have a natural affinity for each other, and there are those which have a quality of strangeness about them. The latter does not mean they do not harmonize but rather that they form a more unusual and intriguing selection of hues. When we refer to the *"natural order of values"* we mean that we have selected the values of the hues used together in the *same order of values* that they are found on the value scale. This does not mean that they must be in these same values. For instance, the normal green is placed at low-light, whereas the normal red falls at high-dark. If we use these two hues together in their natural order of values, all that is meant is that the green would be lighter in value than the red. We would still have a wide range of forms of both hues which could be used together and still select a form of green which would be lighter than the red. We might use a high-light green with a low-light red—or a high-light green with a low-dark red. So long as the green is lighter than the red, it would be natural order of values.

If we reverse those values and use the red lighter than the green, then it becomes *"reverse order of values,"* and we find that they do not have that natural affinity for each other and need to be planned more carefully. To illustrate, we might use an example far removed from the subject of color. Not all persons get along well together. They may clash because of personality differences, their personal interests may be so different that they have no common interests, they may have racial prejudices. Whatever the reasons for their disagreements, they may still live together in the same community and get along with each other in peace providing they observe certain courtesies. They may see each other only occasionally and thus be able to keep from getting on each other's nerves. Or their interests may be so different that they appeal to each other even more because of their differences. With our color combinations of reverse order of values, one way to make them harmonize—or get along well together—is to use only a small amount of the reverse value with a large amount of the other colors, or have the values and intensities decidedly different from each other. When they are so similar, they may be just enough different to compete for attention and spoil the whole effect of harmony. Reverse order of value may be more effective when more hues are used in one design.

Reverse order of values can also be compared to dissonance in music. Frequently a melody in minor key is much more haunting and beautiful than one in a more ordinary major key. The technique of singing or playing a musical instrument in a minor key takes more skill to know just how much off-key to pitch a note and have it sound "right." Contemporary composers of music by using dissonance to produce a "just right" off-key combination of tones give a dramatic, intriguing, or haunting quality. This is a drastic change from compositions of the past such as a Strauss waltz. These compositions were developed around major key sounds. In music, to a person whose ear is not attuned to the appreciation of dissonance the sounds may appear as discord. In color, a combination of hues in reverse order of values may in turn appear as discord to the person who is not sensitive to the dramatic possibilities of these "off-key" hues.

If one has a thorough understanding of the dimension of value, he should be able to:

1. Name the steps on the standard value scale with the equivalent normal hues in relation to them.
2. Raise or lower the value of any hue.
3. Identify the step on the value scale to which a hue has been changed.
4. Identify the value key which has been used in a composition.

INTENSITY

The third dimension of color is intensity or chroma—the variation in brightness and dullness—its strength or its weakness. Value is the dimension which enables a color to speak in a very dainty, quiet manner, or in a heavy, gentlemanly tone. Intensity is the property that enables it to shout in a shrill, vibrant tone or in a quiet, dignified, or somber manner. The normal hues are the ones which are the brightest that it is possible for a color to be. The grayed forms are the ones which are closer to the neutral. To lower the intensity we can add the complement which is the color directly across from it, the line connecting the two going through the center of the circle, or add a neutral of gray, black, or white. For instance, yellow is the complement of violet; red is the complement of green; yellow-green is the complement of red-violet. When the complement is added to a color, the normal reaction is not only to gray the color but also to make it darker in value. If one wishes to add the complement and keep the value constant, neutral white needs to be added also. As the complement is added to the color, there is a midpoint between the two where the resulting color is a neutral. For example, if one adds green to red to make a dull red, by adding increasing amounts of green we reach the midpoint where both the red and green are destroyed by each other and every other addition of green thereafter would result in a grayed green rather than a grayed red.

The reason the word "complement" is used is because it is derived from the word "complete." For instance, in the complementary combination of red and green we note that red is one of the primary hues. Green is a mixture of blue and yellow, the two other primaries. Thus, in the combination, we have used all three of the primary hues. This is true of each pair of hues which are directly across from each other on the color wheel and which we designate as complementary hues. When we lower or raise the value of a color we can indicate the step on the value scale to which it would be equivalent. Then we would have a relatively good idea of the degree of darkness and lightness of the resulting color. When we lower the intensity of a color, however, we do not have as satisfactory a way of identifying the particular degree of intensity to which the color has been lowered. Through experimentation and practice, we are able to recognize when a color has been grayed only slightly, or made very dull, or various degrees in between. The Prang notation system expresses forms of colors in the following manner:

1. Hue is indicated by the initials of the color as R for red, or YG for yellow-green.

2. Value is indicated by the name of the initials of the step to which it corresponds on the value scale as high-light or HL. Thus red at high-light would be indicated as R HL.

3. Intensity is expressed as a fraction or a percentage of its degree of neutralization, as ¼N or 25%N. Thus a slightly grayed, high-light red would be designated as R HL ¼N, or R HL 25%N. One that is very dull and low-dark might be indicated as R LD ⅞N, or R LD 87%N. (See Fig. 6-6.)

It would be wise for one making a study of color to make a series of graduations of hue, value, and intensity of several hues, and arrange them in a comparative chart. By actually mixing pigments, one can see the reaction which takes place and be able to recognize similar forms of colors already mixed, as in printed fabrics.

Effects of brightness or dullness may be varied by means of different textures. A shiny texture reflects light, whereas a dull one absorbs it. Therefore if two fabrics, a shiny polished cotton and a rough weave cotton boucle, were both put into the same dye bath, the polished cotton would appear brighter in intensity. The rough weave would soften the intensity of the color and make it seem duller. This is one of the reasons why a large person should be careful in choosing a shiny textured fabric, especially in bright intensities. It would make her seem even larger in scale and call attention to her size. Observe packages of meat in the supermarket—the sprigs of green parsley or rings of green pepper make the meat appear more red and delicious.

Law of Areas. To make the most satisfactory color harmonies one must be aware of what is sometimes referred to as the "Law of Areas"—the "Law of Backgrounds." This "Law" states that the largest area should be quiet in effect with small accents of bright intensities. Gradually over many centuries we have become more accustomed to more noise in our surroundings—motors, horns, bells, machines all clammering at once. The more noise we have, the more resistance we build up for it, so that we do not notice the noise. The colors we use in our homes, our advertising, our wearing apparel are gradually showing brighter intensities. What is grayed to us might have seemed bright to former generations. However, in spite of all this, we still follow, in our own relative way, the Law of Areas, especially for color combinations for large areas such as rooms. One of the most common violations of the Law of Areas is our use of equal amounts of bright red and bright green for Christmas decorations. Some people defend this combination because it is traditionally Christmas. Actually the green of Christmas comes from the evergreen which is both a dark and dulled green. The red came from the tiny red berries. The larger areas were then the dark dull green, accented with the small areas of bright red. Nature seems always to follow the Law of Areas.

If one has a thorough understanding of the dimension of intensity, he should be able to:

1. Recognize the forcefulness of bright intensities and use them wisely. Follow the Law of Areas.

2. Change the intensities of colors by the addition of the complement or neutral.

3. Change the intensity of colors and still keep the value constant.

4. Make a color appear to be more intense by placing it beside some of its complementary hue.

5. Make a color appear to be more intense by placing beside it more of the same hue in a duller intensity.

6. Make a color appear to be less intense by placing beside it a very dull related hue about the same value.

MECHANICAL COLOR SCHEMES

Most students of color wish to have some more or less specific starting points for planning their color combinations. We stress the fact that every color in all forms is beautiful. It is just a problem of deciding which form for which purpose and how large an area to use. That, however, is a big order. We may begin by studying other combinations which have been used in pictures, fabrics, homes, store windows, magazines. Many times, however, a color scheme may look beautiful in one place but not be so fine when repeated for the purpose for which we need the colors. Another way to begin might be to divide the color wheel into two main groups: related hues and contrasting hues. We may then plan some subheadings under each of these so our outline would be as follows:

A. Related hues
    1. Monochromatic
    2. Analogous
    3. Accented neutral
B. Contrasting hues
    1. Complementary
        a. Simple complement
        b. Split-complement
        c. Double-complement
    2. Triad

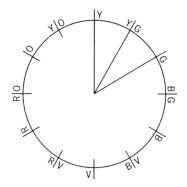

Fig. 6-8. Neighboring hues are analogous.

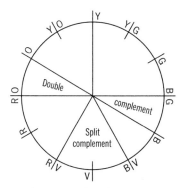

Fig. 6-9. Hues directly across from each other are complementary. (O and B, BG and RO). The four together form a double-complement. The split-complement has one hue with two forms of its complement, as (Y with RV and BV).

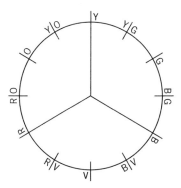

Fig. 6-10. The triad is composed of three hues equally distant, as (R, Y, and B).

Related hues have a color in common. They are classified as the same or similar in hue. "Mono-" means "one" and "chroma" means "color-intensity." Thus a monochromatic color scheme has come to mean different values or intensities of one color. There are a number of suggestions which might aid one in making a more interesting color harmony with only one color, but these suggestions will all be grouped together at the end of this chapter as many of them could be applied to all types of color schemes.

Analogous hues are those which lie next to each other or near each other on the color wheel. They have a color in common. For instance, yellow-green, green, and blue-green all have green in common. We could also say they have yellow in common. If we went further around the color wheel we might add yellow, yellow-orange, and orange and still be able to say they all have yellow in common. However, it is usually wise, for the sake of eliminating the confusion of too many hues in one scheme, to limit the selection of hues to those which lie either between two primaries or two secondaries. (See Fig. 6-8.)

We have already discussed earlier in this chapter the fact that complementary hues are those which lie across from each other on the color wheel, the line connecting them going through the center of the circle. Sometimes, for the sake of variety, we wish to add another hue, or more unusual forms. For instance, instead of using red and green we may wish to use the yellow-green and blue-green on either side of the green with the red. This is referred to as a *split-complement*. When we have need of a still greater variety of hues, two sets of complements, like yellow-green and red-violet, blue-green and red-orange, could be used, and thus classified as a *double-complement*. (See Fig. 6-9.)

Triad hues are those which are equally distant on the color wheel. Each set forms an equilateral triangle, as in red, yellow, blue—green, orange, violet—yellow-green, red-orange, blue-violet—yellow-orange, red-violet, blue-green. (See Fig. 6-10.)

The accented neutral scheme could be classified under related hues because only one hue need be used as the accent for large areas of neutral gray, black, or white. Neutrals are not classified literally as hues. The accented neutral might also be classified under the contrasting color schemes because of the contrast between the hue and the neutral.

Fig. 6-11. Color lends itself in each of the dimensions to expressions of rhythm. This student experiment shows gradations of size, gradation of hues of red-orange, orange, yellow-orange, and black, gradation of values, and also gradation of intensities.

Fig. 6-12. A student experiment for a rug design shows graceful *sweeping rhythms* in a pleasing *gradation of hues* of yellow-orange, orange, and red-orange.

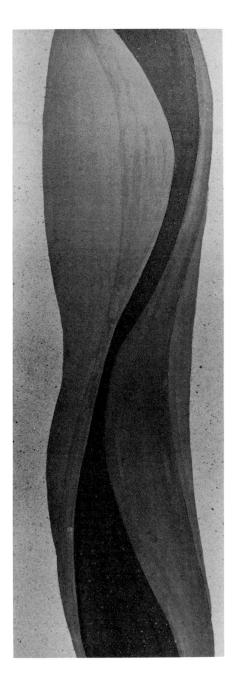

Fig. 6-13. Blue-green and gray have been varied in dark and light for this student rug design. An intermediate-major key is expressed because of the main area of middle values, with smaller areas of light values, and a fine outline of dark values.

Fig. 6-14. Double-complementary hues of yellow-orange and yellow-green with blue-violet and red-violet give a wide variety of values which may be combined in a complex study of values and intensities.

Fig. 6-15. A student experiment with colors and shapes for a rug design successfully expresses a quiet dignity by means of minor contrast of values of grayed blue-green and gray.

SUGGESTIONS FOR PLANNING PLEASING COLOR HARMONIES

Just because we select hues from particular locations on the color wheel is no assurance that the result will be a beautiful color harmony. Two colors have been described as being in harmony when each looks better or happier when viewed together. Each color in a harmony has the effect of making the other color more attractive. Many times one color may seem exciting and enjoyable by itself. However, by placing the color next to another color, it suddenly becomes interesting. The following are suggestions for helping you in planning more pleasing color harmonies:

1. Any combination of colors can be made either pleasant or unpleasant, owing to the choice of values and intensities. For instance, blue and orange may be unattractive and uninteresting if used as they are found on the color wheel. On the other hand, they may be very interesting if both of the colors are dulled somewhat (one dulled more than the other) and also if there is some difference in darkness and lightness.

2. Colors usually appear best when they are kept in the same value relationship as that in which they are found on the value scale (natural order of values). If reverse order of values is used, remember to use contrast of value or intensity, or both, and vary the sizes of the areas.

3. A color harmony should have a dominant color, light or dark effect, warm or cool effect, and/or a combination of these.

4. Dulled warm colors generally are a better background than are cool colors, because warm colors seem to draw together and unify colors placed against them. Cool colors as backgrounds seem to separate colors placed against them.

5. Background colors should follow the principle of the Law of Areas. Intense colors should be used as small accents. The smaller the area, the brighter their color may be.

6. All light values which are also all rather bright are apt to give a very weak, immature, and uninteresting effect. When all dark values are used together the result may appear depressing and old.

7. A very bright color and a very dull color, both the same value, are seldom very attractive when used together. (The bright color will often

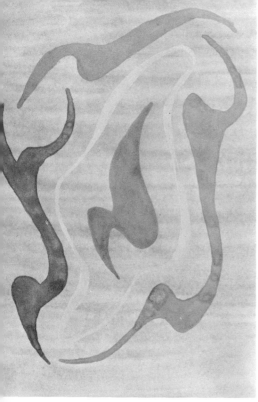

A

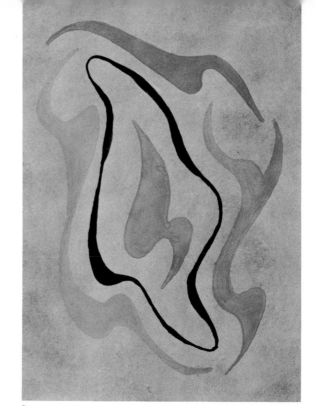

B

C

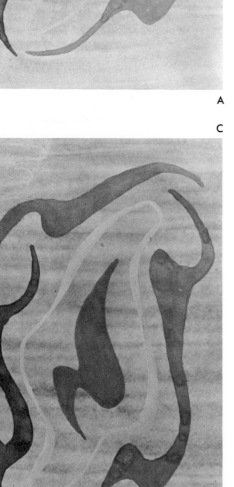

Fig. 6-16. The same design and the same hues may be varied in values and intensities for entirely different effects. Green, blue-green, and blue were the hues used in these experiments.

A. More closely related values expressing a high minor key.

B. Contrasting values of neighboring hues in a high-major key.

C. A moderate contrast of values using an intermediate range of values.

look unrefined and garish, whereas the dull color will seem muddy and drab.)

8. A group of colors in which all colors are of pure intensity (even though some variety in darkness and lightness may be present) often looks unrefined and primitive.

9. The more contrast there is in value, the more "exciting" and "dramatic" the combinations. When too much contrast is used, however, the result is apt to be confusing and lacking in unity.

10. When it is impossible to match exactly the color of the items, a decided contrast is preferable to two similar colors.

CREATIVE EXPERIMENTS

1. To develop an awareness of color in everyday surroundings:
   a. Check through the "color glossary" at the end of this book and find in magazines as many examples as you can of color combinations illustrating the terms in the glossary.
   b. Find examples of color combinations which illustrate the following words: melancholy, gaiety, anger, quietness.
2. To experiment with color in a creative manner:
   a. Make a chart to show examples of change of hue, value, and intensity.
   b. Use colored papers and plan three small abstract designs.
      (1) Repeat the design four times on one plate illustrating:
         (a) Related hues
         (b) Contrasting hues
         (c) Warm hues
         (d) Cool hues
      (2) Repeat the second design four times on one plate illustrating:
         (a) High major key
         (b) High minor key
         (c) Low major key
         (d) Low minor key

    (3) Repeat the third design four times on one plate illustrating:
        (*a*) Bright intensities
        (*b*) Dull intensities
        (*c*) Slightly grayed intensities
        (*d*) Law of areas

c. Plan a composition expressing rhythm and paint it, using different values of one color.

d. Repeat the design in (*c*) using different values of related hues.

e. Plan a simple geometric design and trace it four times. Paint each to illustrate:
    (1) Related hues and related values
    (2) Related hues and contrasting values
    (3) Complementary hues and reverse order of values
    (4) Triad hues and law of areas

f. Plan a simple abstract design to suggest modern industry. Select colors which will carry out the theme of the design.

g. Listen to a record and let the melody suggest a design. Complete the design with colors which carry out the theme of the music.

128

7

FEELING IS SEEING

Sales personnel are urged by their employers to "get the merchandise into the customer's hands—let her *feel* it." Feeling is seeing. A desire for the article grows stronger as she handles it, views it from all angles, imagines it in her own home. Students in foreign lands are frequently blindfolded and required to feel objects of art or feel them under a protective covering of cloth so there will not be the temptation to look at the object at the same time they feel it. Thus the tactile sense is developed to a high degree, and as a result the visual sense is also strengthened. We refer to depth, width, and height of a form; the hue, value, and intensity of a color. Differences in texture can be referred to as smooth, rough, slippery, soft, silky, fuzzy, sharp, and many other adjectives as we become more aware of the variations of the surfaces which we touch.

Youngsters are constantly cautioned by their elders, "Don't touch;" whereas if they were taught *how* to touch, they would develop an appreciation early in life for all phases of beauty.

TEXTURE VERSUS PATTERN VERSUS FORM

It may be interesting to try to distinguish just where texture, pattern, and form begin and end. For instance, a brick has a certain roughness about it when we run a hand over its surface. A brick wall which has had the bricks arranged in a particular manner might take on a pattern of long and short areas, with the mortar between giving a variation in the height of the larger surface. Occasionally the bricklayer might place the form of a whole brick in a projecting manner for additional individuality. In doing so, the regularity of pattern is changed, but so is the texture of the entire wall area.

An airplane view of a plowed field may give an impression of ridges and undulating irregularities in the surface contour of the field. As we fly closer to the field we can discern the pattern made by the furrows on the flat areas and on the slopes. As we walk in the field we are conscious of the degree of the angle of slope in the furrows, the shapes of the leaves of the plants growing in the field. Thus we see that the study of texture is a relative one and is closely linked with the study of all the other elements: line, shape, form, color, and space.

In general, we say that texture is the surface quality of an object. It deals most directly with the sense of touch, although we *see* much more on the surface because we are aware of how it *feels*. A cabinetmaker runs his hand over a piece of furniture to determine its quality by the finish that has been given to it. He evaluates the proportions of the shape and the method of construction, but the first and final test is in the feel of the surface. It must feel smooth, hard, and rich. The dressmaker handles the fabric between her fingers, crushes it, lets it fall from her hand in a draping position, gets the feel of the "hand" of the fabric. The particular arrangement of yarns in the weave and the blending of colors are important in the evaluation, but the texture itself can be judged mainly by the feel.

Imagine, if you can, the delicate softness and fluffiness and almost the feeling of "nothingness" of a handful of dacron filler, then the bulky, yet soft handful of cotton, and then run your hand over a piece of spongy foam rubber. Handle a piece of thin crisp tracing paper, a heavier piece of typing paper of good quality, and a piece of cheap mimeograph paper, and then a piece of lightweight cardboard with a pebbly surface like mat board. We could go on like this, listing hundreds of textures, each with a different surface feel and appearance. These few will suffice to start one thinking of the importance of this element in planning a design.

During this past generation we have become acquainted with the term "honest expression in the use of materials." Manufacturers have created a host of new materials in the synthetic field. The first reaction to many of them by the average consumer was a negative one unless the material or the article made from it reminded the consumer of that which he was already familiar. But individuals with a sense of integrity and imagination could see the new materials had great promise and wished to see them used in the best ways possible, not just in imitation of old materials. The early makers of linoleum surfaces for floors frequently imitated the design of the grain of wood and printed it on the linoleum. Or painters used a skillful maneuvering of the brush to simulate the grain of wood when covering a painted area. Celluloid manufacturers created the effect of ivory. Hard plastic surfaces today frequently give the effect of wood grain, but it is no longer painted on the surface in imitation but is photographed from the actual wood surface. Thus the consumer has the design and the warmth of the grain of the wood, and also has the advantages of the hard plastic which does not scar, mar, stain, and can be easily cleaned.

Architects and builders appreciate the value of texture to enhance their designs. The early builders exposed the beams in ceilings because it was the quickest and easiest method of construction. They had the choice of the best materials in the uncut forests and consequently the beams deserved to show. As the building industry expanded and materials became more expensive and more scarce, building methods were developed to utilize less expensive materials, covering them with plaster, paint, or wallpaper. We still do this today, of course, but there is also a return to the early idea of exposing building materials and making them a definite part of the decorative pattern of the building. Charles Eames was one of the pioneers. His own home in California is an excellent example of the use of exposed metal framework for both the interior and exterior of the house. Cement blocks are used extensively in many areas for wall construction, letting the rough texture of the blocks form the pattern for both interior and exterior walls. The size and shape of the blocks which are assembled as well as the designs of the molds can be varied in many ways to produce beautiful patterns and textures.

Landscape architects have learned much from the Oriental gardeners concerning the use of natural textures in their compositions. We know that the straight cement walks, the precisely shaped and trimmed shrubs, trees, and lawns may be the more formal and most easily cared for garden. But the rugged beauty of natural rock formations or the casualness of flat discs of wood cut from tree trunks and used for stepping stones or terrace adds more natural beauty of texture to a garden.

Early painters used their paint in a very smooth, precise manner, but contemporary painters go beyond this. They do not hesitate to use their paint smooth if they wish to create a particular effect, but they also are not afraid to experiment with other ways of using a medium to produce other effects. They may put it on thick with a palette knife, with their fingers, or dab it with a sponge or paper towel, or crush a wire mesh screen on the surface. These textural effects offer wide possibilities for the painter to express himself in whatever way he chooses.

VISUAL REPRESENTATION OF TEXTURES

The above paragraphs discuss the way a painter may produce actual textures on the surface of his canvas, but the painter may also be concerned with simulating or representing textures in his composition. For instance, if he is painting a portrait, he will wish to show the flesh tones, the texture of the hair, the crisp, filmy, velvety, or wooly texture of the fabric on the model. This representation of various textures is not to be confused with the lack of honesty in the use of materials as discussed earlier in this chapter. Imitation for the sake of producing an article less expensively is a discredit to any designer.

A painter or commercial artist may be concerned with another aspect of representation of texture—that of the effect of light on a surface. The surface color is broken up by many minute gradations of light and shadow which arrange themselves differently on various textures.

1. Dull or rough textures such as wool or cotton surfaces, wood or stone, absorb light and have an arrangement of closely related values in the light and shadow, representing a high, intermediate, or low minor key.

2. Shiny or smooth textures, such as satin, polished metal, or glass, reflect light and have an arrangement of strong contrast of values in the light and shadow, representing a high major key.

3. Pile fabrics like velvet or corduroy both reflect and absorb light. The arrangement of light and shadow represent a low major key. Every thread of the pile is casting a little shadow on its neighbor so that the reflection on the surface is limited to the topmost tips of the pile.

COMBINATIONS OF TEXTURES

There are no rigid rules or laws concerning the combination of correct textures. One needs to develop a sensitivity to those textures which seem to have a natural affinity for each other. Textures should have something in common or be a pleasant contrast. They may have an air of informality, as an arrangement of zinnias in a copper bowl, placed on a burlap cloth. They may express dainty formality for a reception when an arrangement of iris and tulips in a glass container are placed on an organdy cloth. In each instance the textures seem to repeat the same character. There might, however, be a feeling of interesting contrast such as an interior wall which exposes the natural brick flanked on one side with a window area which is covered with folding panels of opaque plastic in wooden frames like a shojii screen. On the other side of the brick wall might be a solid color drapery of a smooth but not shiny cotton weave. The wood paneling in the built-in cabinets nearby show the fine grain of mahogony rubbed to a rich smoothness. Only the tweed carpeting repeats the roughness of the brick. But there is a feeling of correctness about the whole combination, for the textures are selected and used in a natural way to show off each of the areas to satisfaction. Textures should be selected for harmony of idea or for the use that is to be made of them rather than for their similarity or contrast.

CREATIVE EXPERIMENTS

1. Experiments to develop an awareness of textures:
   a. Collect a group of actual textures and group in gradations of smooth to rough, thick to thin, heavy to light, etc. These might be all fabrics, or all leaves, or all pieces of bark, or whatever way you wish to collect and group them.

    b. Collect a group of simulated textures from magazines or other sources and classify them in similar ways to (*a*).

    c. Collect groups of textures which may be quite different (like satin, fine kid, and pearls) but seem to have a natural affinity for each other or which we may associate together for a particular purpose.

2. Experiment with creating textural effects or compositions utilizing a variety of textures:

    a. Use finger paint and experiment with a variety of techniques of creating textural effects: with fingers, hand, arm, brush, palette knife, comb, sponge, wire mesh, and many other tools.

    b. Create an abstract collage of a variety of textures which harmonize or contrast satisfactorily with each other.

    c. Use different materials, such as clay, plaster, wood, moist sand, metal foil or leather, and shape, carve, or tool textural effects in the surface.

Fig. 7-1. Textures of some woods become very rough and linear in character as the branch is exposed to the ravages of wind and rain.

Fig. 7-2. Textures of other woods are smooth and polished, resembling the leathery skin of an elderly individual who has spent many years in the out-of-doors.

Fig. 7-3. Wood shavings and sawdust have a brittle or crumbly texture.

Fig. 7-4. Some tree barks are extremely rough, deeply ridged, and hard to the touch.

Fig. 7-5. Other bark textures are less rough and ridged and show small areas of smoothness which contrast with the roughness.

Fig. 7-6. Metal is usually thought of as being hard, slick, and smooth. However, when the brass is melted with a welding torch, it assumes a polished roughness which may reflect a similar response as caused by the bark of the tree in Fig. 7-5.

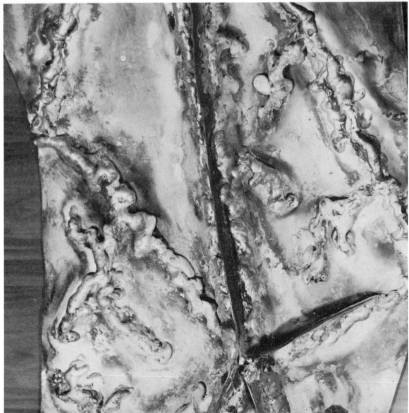

Fig. 7-7. The soft furry ears are contrasted with the sharpness of the texture of the grass. ("Princess," owner, Letta Lockhart.)

Fig. 7-8.   A combination of textures represented by the riblike veins of the canna leaf enhanced by the crystal-like drops of dew.   The shadow pattern in the background also gives a softened texture of high-lights and shadows.

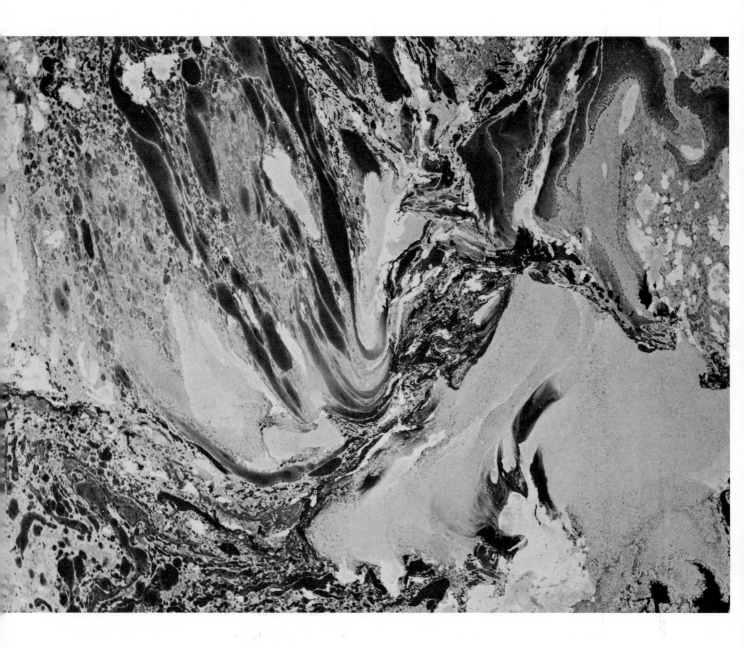

Fig. 7-9.   Immersing a sheet of paper into water on which oil paint has been floated gives a marbleized texture on the paper.   Although the results may be quite uncertain, the colors and textures can be very exciting.

Fig. 7-10. A, B, and C: A variety of textures obtained in Yucatan Stone. (Photographs courtesy of Murals, Inc.) D. Carved firebrick shows similar roughness of texture of the Yucatan Stone.

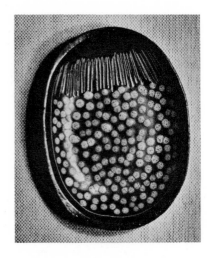

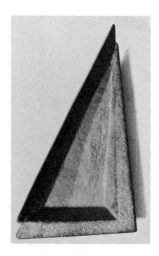

(upper left)
Fig. 7-11. Experimentation with techniques of applying glazes creates unusual textures. (Designers, Jane and Gordon Martz. Courtesy of Marshall Studios, Inc.)

(upper right)
Fig. 7-12. Cast iron may be left rough or relatively smooth for contrast of textures. (Photograph courtesy of Design Today, Inc.)

Fig. 7-13. Techniques of casting plaster in semiflat designs may give variety of texture in the background with the smoothly rounded bird forms. (Photograph courtesy of Design Today, Inc.)

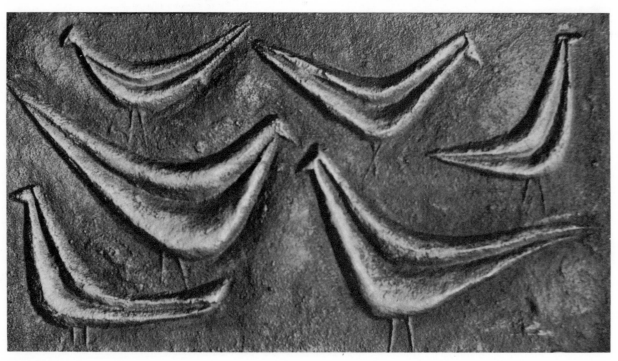

Fig. 7-14. The texture of the highly glazed tiles lend themselves dramatically to strong contrasts of dark and light. (Designed by Evelyn Ackerman for Era Industries.)

Fig. 7-15. The uncut loops of yarn give a "seedlike" texture to the hooked rug. (Photograph "Seed Pods," Courtesy of Era Industries. Designer, Evelyn Ackerman.)

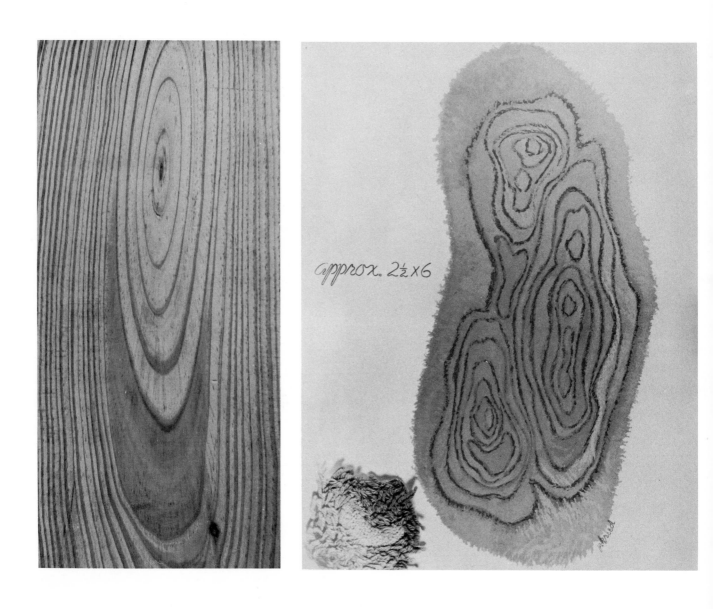

approx. 2½ × 6

Fig. 7-16.   Smoothly rounded ovals in the grain pattern of wood may suggest to the designer similar patterns to be adapted for rhythmical rug designs.

Fig. 7-17. Seed "paintings" of red, yellow, shelled, and dyed millet, poppy-seeds and rape-seeds give colorful textural effects for simple, dramatic abstract composition such as the "Bird" and "Still Life" by R. Bushong. (Photographs courtesy of Tom Tru Corp.)

Fig. 7-18. The textured background emphasizes the figures and also creates a contrast in color pattern. (Photograph courtesy of Design Today, Inc.)

Fig. 7-19. The dramatic textures of the ceramic tiles add interest to the related shapes. (Designed by Fran Williams. Made by Marnay Ltd. Owner, Martye Poindexter.)

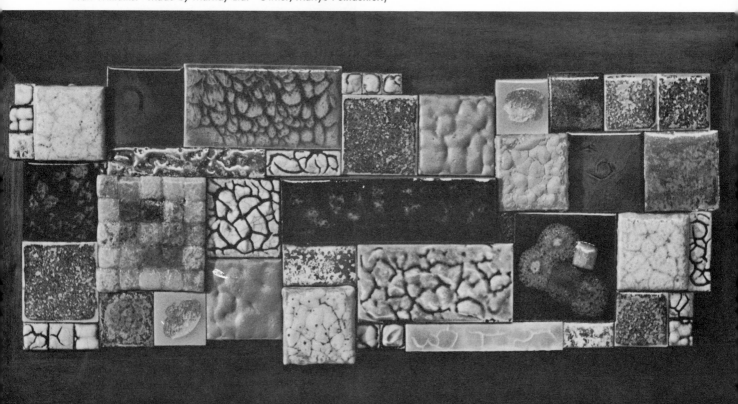

Fig. 7-20. What textural effects are suggested to you when you use a felt pen? Are they rough, fuzzy, delicate, heavy, thick, thin, sharp, smooth? Try a variety of tools and materials to see what different textural effects you can achieve.

A

Fig. 7-21. Materials such as finger paint lend themselves to a variety of textural effects, depending upon the techniques used. In (A) the paint has been put on thick in a wavy pattern and then a brush was used to create the textured effect.

In (B) the fingers were used to create the thick textured effect.

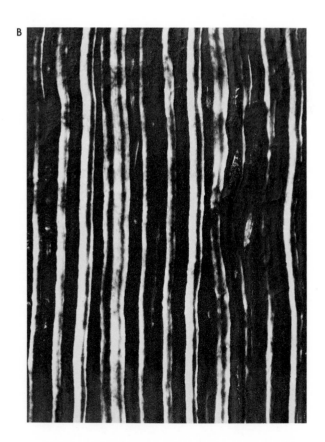

B

A

B

Fig. 7-22. Oil paint (A) and transparent water color (B) create very different effects. Oil paint is thick and opaque and lends itself to rough textured effects. Water color is thin and transparent and creates a watery effect on the background.

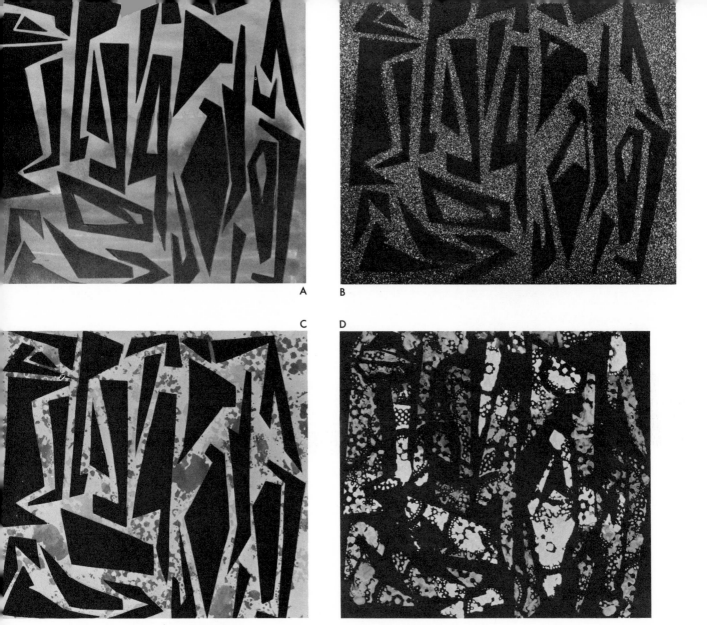

Fig. 7-23.   Designs take on an entirely different effect sometimes when various textures are used.   A. The background was blended softly with transparent water color.   B. A spattered effect of opaque white was used, creating a "sandpaper" texture.   C. A mottled background was created with a sponge, whereas in (D) a piece of all-over lace was used for the stenciled shapes, creating a very rough, decorative, textural effect.

8

DESIGNING WITH THE ABC'S

The major purpose of this textbook has been to help you in your use of the principles of design to develop a more sensitive organization of the elements. For study purposes each chapter has centered around the use of the design principles as mainly related to one element. Your success or growth is reflected in your ability to combine these individual elements. Every time you make design judgements you reflect your understanding of design. You may choose to do a piece of sculpture, a painting, a piece of jewelry, design or even select an ensemble, design a piece of furniture, plan a room, or select an everyday object that you use.

A poster that you design will also show evidence of your sensitivity to design. Actually you can develop a poster with only a few simple technical skills. Through work with many students we have chosen posters as one way of looking at design understanding. This chapter dealing with lettering is planned to prepare you to develop a poster. Most college art departments offer lettering courses and this book is not intended to be a substitute for these courses. A high degree of skill and technique, produced by much practice and study, is needed before you can become proficient in lettering.

Cave painting and hieroglyphics evidenced man's early desire to use a form of written communication. As man's society has become more complex, his need to rely on written communication has become increasingly

Fig. 8-1. Variety in the style of lettering as well as variation in size helps to call attention to the main idea. (Photograph courtesy of the Department of Public Information, Ottawa, Canada.)

important. From the early drawings and symbols, our present-day written language has evolved. Although you have developed the written word to a point where you can convey ideas in various ways, by using an understanding of design you can increase your effectiveness in written communication. It is discouraging to receive a letter from a friend and not be able to decipher it. It is equally important to have written instruction or advertisements which are expressive. By applying our understanding of design, we will attempt to make our written words more communicative.

The prime purpose of all lettering is to be functional. When observed the lettering not only must be readable, but easily so. Many times when you are writing a theme you may spell incorrectly a simple word several times. But it may be difficult for you to discover this glowing error. The same thing holds true for your lettering. It is easy for you to read because you know what you intended to say. But can you still read it when it is "cold"? There is a story of a person who had written instructions for an employee. The employee failed to carry out instructions much to the dismay of the employer. The employee simply could not read the instructions and brought them back to this boss. The boss examined the instructions carefully for several minutes and replied, "I could read it if I could remember what I had said."

For lettering to be effective there must be consistency. Obviously in posters and advertising we break this consistency for certain words or phrases so they may draw special attention. (See Fig. 8-1.) However, this must be handled with care to keep from creating confusion.

The most obvious inconsistency in lettering is in the letter "I." In present-day lettering we have most often omitted serifs, commonly called "feet," except in the letter "I." If all letters carry serifs, then you have the beginning of consistency, but when you use these only on one or two letters, these letters tend to draw too much attention. Even so, there are times when consistency may be in conflict with functionalism. How would you letter the abbreviation of Illinois? In your own lettering, do you have a consistent placement of crossbars, as well as in your circles and straight lines? Have you developed the best possible consistency for readability? Can you be objective about this? Or do you need someone else to examine your lettering?

Greater readability can be gained through the character or personality

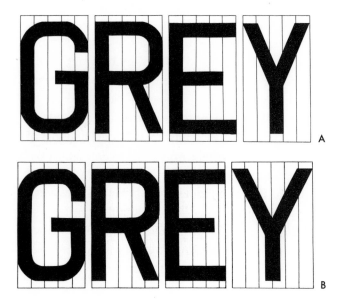

A

B

Fig. 8-2. In (A) the letters each occupy the same amount of space, thus causing the E to look large and the Y to appear small. In (B) the E was reduced in size and the Y made larger to give a semblance of the same size.

TORN

SOLID

Fig. 8-3. The words take on personality or character to reflect the meaning of the word. For "Torn" the letters have literally been torn and for "Solid" the letters are heavy and bold.

of the lettering. Uniqueness in lettering helps to draw attention, but in no way should it hinder the basic function. This individuality of lettering should be not only an expression of the individual but also the expression of what is being lettered. An example of this could be the personality of lettering used to describe a sheer fabric as compared to the lettering describing concrete. (See Fig. 8-3.) In posters and advertising it is desirable for the important words, phrases, or thoughts to have a distinct character of their own.

In lettering it is desirable to work toward similarity in proportions. However, you may create more design interest by introducing certain variations. Obviously, letters need to appear to occupy the same amount of space within each word. The word "appear" is the key to this thought. If a "W" or "M" is made to occupy the same space as an "H," it would look crowded or pinched. It is equally difficult to have an "I" occupy the same space as an "H," much less an "M" or "W." Although these examples are more obvious, comparing an upper case "E" with an upper case "H" points out a more subtle point. The top, middle, and bottom of the "E" tend to lead your eye to the right, giving this letter the feeling of occupying a larger space. To make the "E" feel as if it occupies as much space as an "H," the "E" needs to be narrowed slightly.

In exploring variations in lettering it is important to be concerned with the placement of the cross bar. In mechanical printing processes the cross bar is usually in the center of the letter. This divides the space above and below equally. More interest can be gained by slightly raising or lowering this cross bar. Not only must we be concerned with the space a letter occupies, we must be aware of the spaces created within the letter, as well as the spaces between the letters.

From a design point of view, one cannot mechanically space letters successfully. There is no formula that can be applied to each letter. The space between an "A" and an "H" will be different than the space between an "A" and a "T." The "A" should actually extend under the arm of the "T." In most communities one is able to find signs that are mechanically spaced and difficult to read. Locally, one large sign has H O T E L. It is actually very readable as HOT EL.

Variation of thickness or thinness in the lines of a letter can create more interest in a word. Various lettering pens and brushes give this variation

LILAC

LILAC

Fig. 8-4.   In A the same mechanical amount of space has been left between each letter, whereas in B the same optical space has been left.

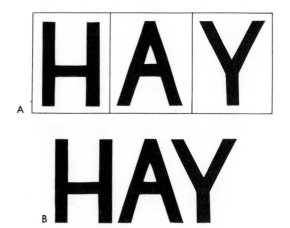

Fig. 8-5.   In A the same mechanical amount of space has been left between each letter, whereas in B the same optical space has been left, thus making it necessary to slightly "overlap" the Y over the A.

**L
I
G
H
T**

naturally. The amount will decide whether the effect is subtle or dramatic.

Often in lettering we try experiments that fail to be effective. (This in no way means not to experiment because by no means are all experiments mistakes. Even when we analyze our errors we have the opportunity to learn.) To be different we sometimes try lettering that does not read from left to right, but from top to bottom or on a diagonal. Few words will read well up and down. In fact some well-known simple words become more difficult to read in this position. (See Fig. 8-6.) Even though the words may be more readable on a diagonal this should be used with caution. If these letters are out of balance they may cause one to assume awkward positions (consciously or unconsciously) in an attempt to recreate balance.

In recent years there has been marked improvement in the design quality of trade-marks, and firm signatures. These show imagination, decorative letters, and symbols to personify the character of the firm represented. (See Figs. 8-7A, B, C, and D.)

Processes always affect the final product. Thus in our practical examination of lettering we need to take a look at the various tools and materials we may use to produce lettering.

When lettering, using a pencil, pen, or brush, it is important to be seated comfortably with both feet on the floor, straight back, and freedom of movement for your arm. Too many of us attempt to write with finger movement. Good lettering comes from good arm movement. Proper selection of materials, tools and the care of these reflect in your lettering. A pen point that is clogged with ink will produce sloppy letters. Expensive tools and materials are not necessary, but good selection is important.

Most professionals use guide lines to space the height of their letters. This may not be necessary, but it takes an outstandingly sharp eye not to use them. With upper case letters, use two guide lines and with lower case, use three. These should be drawn accurately with a ruler and very lightly so they can be removed easily.

When using drawing and inking tools, you should pull the point across the paper and not push it. When you push a tool the point tries to stab or become imbedded in the surface and becomes difficult to produce a flowing line. With drawing and inking tools you should always pull the pen straight down or to the right. A left-handed person would pull the pen down and to the left.

Fig. 8-6. Readability has been reduced to a degree because one has to stop and spell the word in one's mind before reading it.

161

Fig. 8-7A. An abstract symbol and monogram developed for the Trans-Mountain Oil Pipeline Co. (Designed by Walter Landor & Assoc., Industrial Designers, San Francisco, California.)

C. Computer Engineering Associates, Inc. of Pasadena, California use a simple monogram combined with an abstract symbol representing their firm. (Designed by Walter Landor & Assoc. Industrial Designers, San Francisco, California.)

B. Emblem used by the Bozak Sales Company. The triangle symbolizes a loudspeaker, for which they are the dealers. (Photograph courtesy of Bozak Sales Company, Darian, Connecticut.)

D. A simple dramatic lower-case "a" becomes the trademark for the Ansul Chemical Co. (Courtesy of the Ansul Chemical Co., Marinette, Wisconsin.)

Most students seem to prefer to start lettering with a pencil because this is a tool with which they are familiar. First, lay out guide lines for upper case letters and use your pencil to produce the ABC's, striving for consistency and interest in your letters. What difference will a hard or soft lead make? What effect can you obtain with the side of the lead? Now experiment with the lower case letters.

Pen and ink offers many possibilities in lettering. With the wide variety of pen points now being produced, you have unlimited possible designs for the individual letters. Figures 8-8 and 9 show the effect of three different points. Design alphabets using a chisel point, an oval point, and a square point. Many of our new felt pens can be effectively used. These will not have the wide range of tops, but the ink that is dry when you put it on paper has certain advantages.

Brush lettering is basically similar to the pen except that there may be evidenced a more flowing line, and of course can be much larger. The chisel-shaped brush is still the one used most for lettering. Although the brush can produce wonderful effects, it takes much more practice to perfect one's skill with this tool. Furthermore, you need to keep in practice.

Cut paper letters have some real advantages although it takes more time to make them than those made by other means. The major advantage is that your letters are glued down. This gives you an opportunity to cut all your letters and then arrange them. If any one letter does not work well, it can be discarded and a new one cut. Also if the word does not occupy enough space, the letters can be spread out. With drawing and inking tools, all your planning must be done first with no room for mistakes. With cut letters, later discovered mistakes can easily be corrected. There are many approaches to cutting letters. One method depends on folding, and another method on cutting all letters open. (See Figs. 8-10 and 11.)

CREATIVE EXPERIMENTS

1. To develop an awareness for beautiful lettering and printing:
    a. Find in magazines or newspapers examples of pleasingly proportioned letters—single letters, monograms or trademarks, whole words, as in "signatures" of firms.

HJKLMNO

GHJKLM

UVWXYZ

Where a curve is combined with a straight line to form a single stroke — pause slightly at their junction without lifting pen to insure a well formed element.

$1234567 89¢

LETTERED WITH STYLE 'B' ROUND TIP PENS

hijklpyq

uvwx&z

VWXY&ZS

SQUEEZED HEADLINE

ABCDEFGIJL

KMNOPQRS

TUVWXYZ?
&

$123456789

AGHJKMNQRSWXY¢

Fig. 8-8A.   Using a round nibbed pen, fine or heavy, the letters become the same thickness throughout and have a rounded feeling about them.   (Reproduced from the 17th Edition of Speedball Text Book, by Ross F. George.   Courtesy of Hunt Pen Co.)

B. By drawing the pen around each part of the letter, the stroke is the same thickness throughout.   This technique may also be used to make the letters more broad than they are tall.   (Reproduced from the 17th Edition of Speedball Text Book, by Ross F. George.   Courtesy of Hunt Pen Co.)

SINGLE-STROKE ROMAN

ABCDE
FGHIJK
LMNOP
QRSTU
VWXYJ
Z&R?ST

Use the size of pen that will make the widest elements in one stroke

19

Style 'C' Speedball Pen Roman

A rapid legible alphabet for Artists and Sho-card Writers.

abcdefg
hijklmno
pqrstuv
wxyz&a
$12345¢
67890

Fig. 8-9A. A chisel-type pen is used for the above "Single Stroke Roman" lettering. The arrows indicate the direction of the strokes. The pen is always held at the same angle so the strokes are thick and thin. (Reproduced from the 17th Edition of Speedball Text Book, by Ross F. George. Courtesy of Hunt Pen Co.)

B. Lower case letters to harmonize with the Single Stroke Roman lettering. Note the proportions within the letters so guide lines may be properly ruled. (Reproduced from the 17th Edition of Speedball Text Book, by Ross F. George. Courtesy of Hunt Pen Co.)

Fig. 8-10A. The grey lines show where to fold the paper vertically and horizontally. B. The grey line on the left shows where to cut for a basic shape. C. The paper is unfolded to show the basic shape which results. Many letters may be cut from this shape. D. A letter "S" may be made from the basic shape by rounding the corners.

Fig. 8-11. Letters may be cut without folding, by cutting into a shape as indicated by the black lines. By this method, letters showing more variation in proportion may be cut.

    b. Divide the examples in (*a*) into those which appear to have been set up in type and those which were no doubt hand lettered before the plate was made for reproduction purposes.

2. To develop skill in designing with letters:

    a. Prepare a plate with a variety of guide lines showing different amounts of space between for various heights of letters. (⅛ inch, ¼ inch, ½ inch, 1 inch.) Some rows of lettering might be provided with two guide lines for capitals and some with three for lower case letters.

    b. Using a pencil, and then your lettering pens, make a series of practice strokes of vertical lines, diagonals, and curves similar to those which you might use in making letters.

    c. Start lettering all the "straight-line" letters first (E, F, H, I, L, T); next do the ones with diagonal lines (A, K, M, N, V, W, X, Y, Z); lastly do the ones with a combination of straight and curved lines (B, D, G, J, P, R, U): and the all-curved ones (C, O, Q, S).

    d. After you have developed sufficient skill in making capitals in a variety of proportions (tall and thin, short and wide, two-thirds as wide as tall) practice making lower case letters (also in a variety of proportions).

    e. Plan a plate in which you choose one letter and practice varying the proportion of the letter in as many ways as you can. Use this letter in a five or six letter word, making the word occupy the same amount of space each time, but vary the proportion of the letters and the spaces between.

    f. Plan an all-over pattern using a group of letters as the decorative motif which is repeated for the pattern.

    g. Choose a poem or a motto and arrange it on a plate in a pleasing manner.

    h. Choose one letter and cut it in a variety of proportions. Arrange them on a page in an interesting way.

    i. Choose one word (four or five letters) and cut the letters so one arrangement of the letters has been made using tall, thin letters, and the other arrangement uses broad, squatty letters.

    j. Choose one word that suggests a certain personality or character. Cut letters which reflect this personality.

9

DESIGN SPEAKS OUT

For the purpose of study you have been introduced separately to the elements of design: line, shape, space, color, and texture. This individual examination was planned to help you to become better acquainted with and to develop a greater sensitivity to each design element. However, in design or in a particular design each element must be viewed in its inter-relationship to other elements. One design may depend mostly on line, but for the design to have quality the spaces between the lines must be examined. Thus the element of space has entered. Also contrast between the line and background must be present for the lines to be visible. This contrast may be in color, (hue, value or intensity), in texture, or in a combination of these. Therefore, the success of a design cannot depend independently on any one element but on the sum total of those used.

Your understanding of design depends on your knowledge and skills in using the guideposts of design to achieve the best organization of the design elements. Every time you work with design you are placed in the position of combining the design elements. However, we have selected posters as a project which lends itself easily to the combining of your design skills and knowledges.

What is the purpose of a poster? The basic purpose can be described as being the communication of information. This information may be

THE TORCH; BE YOURS TO HOLD IT HIGH!
IF YE BREAK FAITH WITH US WHO DIE
WE SHALL NOT SLEEP, THOUGH POPPIES GROW
IN FLANDERS FIELDS.

McCREA.

Fig. 9-1. Illustration dominates the lettering in the Canadian war poster. The tall skyscrapers intensify the upward sweep, and the diagonal rays draw the attention back to the wording. The simplified pattern of dark and light in the human figure adds a still further dramatic touch. (Courtesy of the Director of Public Information, Ottawa, Canada.)

Fig. 9-2. The illustration dominates the lettering to a certain degree, but the symbol for the illustration was chosen wisely to emphasize the slogan, "It's got to fit . . ." (Courtesy of the Director of Public Information, Ottawa, Canada.)

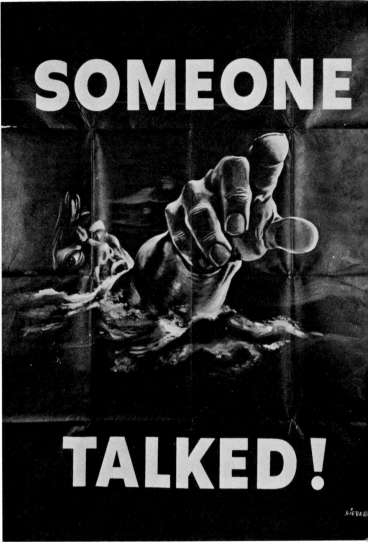

Fig. 9-3. A forceful message to show that the little man who would be least obvious has been responsible for much loss. A national winner in the National War Poster Competition held under auspices of Artists for Victory, Inc., Council for Democracy, Museum of Modern Art. (Collection of the Museum of Modern Art, New York.)

Fig. 9-4. The surrealistic illustration is dominated by the bold block letters in a strong contrast of dark and light. (Designer, Siebel. Photograph courtesy of the U. S. Government Printing Office.)

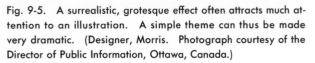

Fig. 9-5. A surrealistic, grotesque effect often attracts much attention to an illustration. A simple theme can thus be made very dramatic. (Designer, Morris. Photograph courtesy of the Director of Public Information, Ottawa, Canada.)

Fig. 9-6. The optical illusion that the smokestacks are "Big Guns" emphasizes strongly the value of contributing to the war effort on the "Home Front." (Photograph courtesy of the Director of Public Information, Ottawa, Canada. Designer, Trevor.)

further described as the expressing of a product, a service, or an idea. Readability and eye appeal are related to the function of a poster. Good design is an integral part of the poster's ability to communicate. The quality of a poster depends on the quality of the design. Thus "design speaks out" through posters.

In recent years we have begun to be more aware of the fact that posters can truly be a work of art. Toulouse-Lautrec's posters are valued for their art quality. Today more and more reproductions of posters are being used on the walls of our contemporary homes. World War II produced many excellent posters to stimulate our maximum patriotic duty. More commercial companies are striving to use top-flight design in their posters and advertising, realizing that good taste in design is an integral part of selling their product.

In developing a poster, you must start with the information you wish to communicate. As an example we will use an announcement that often appears on most campuses.

The Freshman Class with the co-operation of the Student Union will have an all freshman dance. This affair will be semiformal. No admission will be charged. A college group of musicians, The Campus Combo, will provide the music. This dance will be held in the Student Union Ballroom on Friday, November 13, from 8:30 until 11:00. This is a stag or drag affair.

How can we most effectively communicate the information with a poster? Shall we sell our attraction with lettering or illustration? These two should not compete for attention. Travel and bullfight posters have usually depended upon illustration. However, we have found that there are certain disadvantages to stressing illustration in our classes. Many students have not had their basic courses in drawing, and in a short time they do not have the skill to perfect their ability in this field. With illustration too much detail and realism will many times detract. Design quality should take precedence over realism. Simplify, distort, or change the illustration to make it more effective.

Only simple skills are needed to make lettering stand out and be effective. These skills can be reasonably controlled in a short period of time. Many students are able to be more effective with their designs when lettering receives more emphasis than illustration. However, each student must

Fig. 9-7. A student poster which uses lettering as its main center of interest. The act of cutting off corners in this way can be very distracting, however.

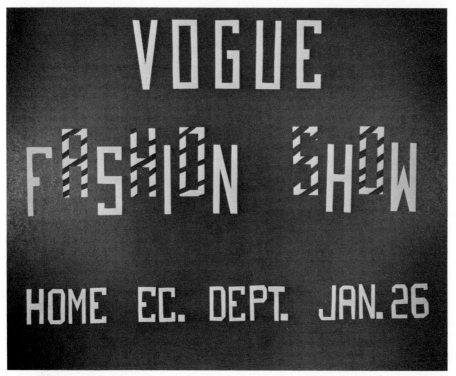

Fig. 9-8. A student poster which uses lettering rather than illustration for its center of interest. The diagonal stripes in alternate letters in "Fashion Show," however, cause those particular letters to fade into the background and make the words difficult to read. Accuracy in identification is also important. Instead of Home Ec. Dept., The School of Home Economics should have been used. Abbreviations should also be consistent.

make his own decision. With your skills and ability, which approach will help you to convey better the information concerning the freshman dance?

Whether you work with lettering or illustration you must strive for readability. You may work toward the readability of thought through words or illustrations. It has often been said that "He who runs can read," and this is a good test for a poster. A poster should never be confused with a newspaper. It is important to select carefully the basic thoughts in their proper order. We all have heard long-winded speakers who make many points. Later we have a hard time remembering any one point. This can be especially true of posters. One poster we recently viewed contained 157 words. Remember, he who says too much will say nothing.

By expressing only two or three points about the freshman dance, what would you choose as being of first importance? Of secondary importance? Do you need to say that all freshmen are invited to the freshman dance? Or does Freshman Dance imply this? Maybe other words will be more effective than "dance." What about the word "Stomp," "Jump," or others which may stand out more for your school? This brings up another point. Who will be your audience? What are the particular characteristics of your group that will be different? How much should these differences be considered in the designing of a poster? Would a poster that advertises a carnival for the elementary school students, for high school students, and one for college students be different? Some would say, "no," because all of us become youngsters when involved with a carnival. However, it becomes obvious that with many activities the interest of our audience will vary greatly.

In the chapter on lettering we have talked about personality of letters. For any poster, it is important to use lettering which characterizes the information. Would there be a difference in the lettering used to tell about a new exciting perfume and the excitement of a circus? There are no set rules that will tell you what lettering to use. Each of you must decide on lettering that will best carry your information. How would you personify letters to carry best the information for our dance poster?

Posters affect the viewer's feeling-responses. If they are crowded and uncomfortable, these same feelings can be conveyed to the observer. It is highly desirable not to crowd your poster, unless you are using a theme such as 'claustrophobia" or "trapped." Slanting words or phrases on a poster can cause the viewer unconsciously to lean to recreate balance. This disturbing factor may result in persons subconsciously rejecting the information. On our campus a series of posters became the focus of editorials and letters to the editor of our student newspaper. The extremely brilliant color combinations seemed to produce a strong bilious feeling in the audience. Is it possible for a poster to be extremely disturbing and still be successful?

Variety must enter into your poster. How much depends upon your interpretation of the information. The greater the variety, the greater the dramatic quality. How long the poster will be posted may have bearing on the dramatic quality of the poster. How dramatic should our dance poster be? How much variety in size and shape shall we work toward? Consider the variation not only in lettering but in other shapes and illustrations. What colors shall we select for our poster? If the dance had been given a particular theme, such as Western, Parisian, or Spring, would this affect our color choices? How much variety do you need in hue, value, and intensity? Should various textures be included? What textures lend themselves to our dance?

What materials should we use? Slick paper, rough paper, fabrics, yarns, and sandpaper are only a few of the many textures that may be successfully introduced into posters.

Should our poster be flat or three-dimensional, or a combination? The answer to this and other questions should be based on one point. What will make our poster most effective with the most eye appeal? This will require originality on your part. Just being different will not necessarily make your poster good. Use your guideposts to good design as your final evaluation. Even the most simple poster becomes very complex when viewed from all points of design. However, the more effectively you use design, the more the design will speak out for you.

In the preceding paragraphs concerning the poster for the freshman dance, you have been asked leading questions pertaining to:

1. The lettering versus illustration
2. The readability
3. The audience who reads the poster
4. The personality of the letters
5. The viewer's feeling-responses

6. The degree of dramatic quality, and

7. The materials to be used

In the following paragraphs we shall discuss the above topics in relation to a specific poster or bulletin board display to enable you to evaluate more accurately your own poster designs. (See Fig. 9-9.) In the bulletin board display for the School of Home Economics of Texas Technological College, the lettering has been made more prominent than the illustrations. Although there are many enlarged photographs combined in the display, the lettering is more prominant because of size and amount of space it occupies.

The display is very readable because the letters are not only large scale but are well-spaced, simple block letters. They are neither too crowded nor too far apart for ease of comprehension.

The display lists clearly the information: "The *Community* wants you," "*Business* wants you," "The *School* wants you." To emphasize further these various areas who "want you," the photographs show individuals participating in training activities preparing the student for the community, business, and school.

The display is naturally expected to appeal more to women than to men. The titles in each main area of lettering have been designed with tall and slender letters, thus giving a more graceful, feminine effect to the poster. "Personality" has been instilled in the letters.

The viewer's feeling-responses toward the display should be one of pleasure because of the satisfactory division of space and the application of the principles of design in the organization of both lettering and photographs. The display is divided exactly in the middle, but each side gives the feeling of being approximately the same weight as the other even though different wording and photographs have been assembled. Thus, balance has been achieved.

If one compares the actual display with the diagram indicating the division of space, Fig. 9-10, one can see that the spaces are unevenly divided for more pleasing proportions, but organization has been developed by starting several words, or groups of words, or strips of dark value on a line vertically or horizontally with other words, photographs, or strips of dark value. This simplifies the display, makes it easier to read, and creates a

Fig. 9-9. Organization of a bulletin board display utilizes the same principles as that of making a poster. Accuracy, readability, and pleasing division of space are most important.

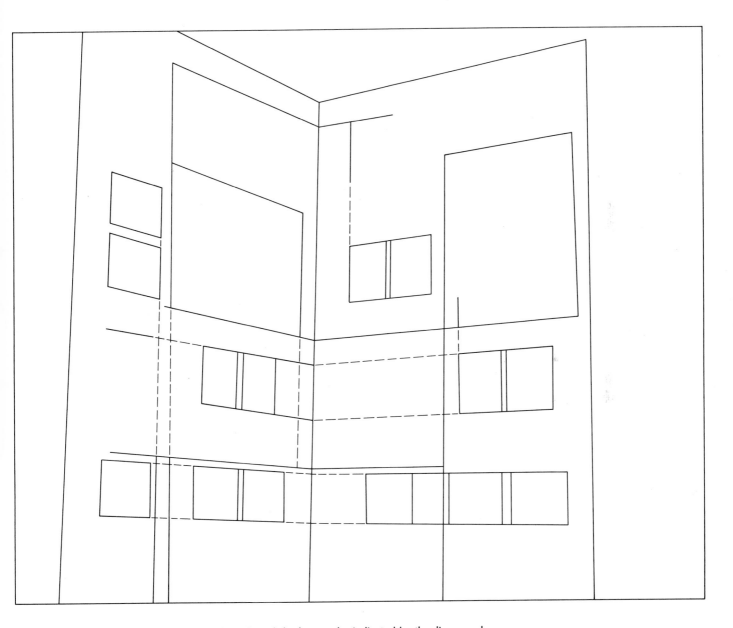

Fig. 9-10. The division of space for the bulletin board display can be indicated by the diagram above to show the use of parallel vertical and horizontal lines or margins to unify the placement of photographs and lettering.

more dramatic quality. Confusion is eliminated because all lines emphasize or reflect the structural or actual shape of the panel on which the display is organized.

The display is further dramatized by means of plain areas used as rest spaces for the eyes, heavy dark strips which lead the attention to specific features, and small light dots on dark backgrounds to emphasize further certain features. The photographs have been grouped close together in strategic areas, with no more than two in any group for ease in identification. The grouping of photographs in pairs also lends a rhythmic quality to the composition.

Commercial cardboard letters have been used for the main headings at the top of each panel, whereas painted letters made with a flat lettering brush have been used for the rest of the lettering. Bright strips of gaily colored cardboard lend a satisfactory variety of materials and tools used. A bulletin board display's speaking power is directly related to the student's satisfactory application of the principles of design.

C R E A T I V E   E X P E R I M E N T S

1. To develop awareness of well-designed posters or advertising:
   a. Find examples of posters or advertising which depend mainly on illustration for their effectiveness.
   b. Find examples which depend mainly on wording for their effectiveness.
   c. Find examples where the total effect of the poster or advertisement reflects the personality or character of the product, service, or idea.

2. To experiment with creating a poster:
   a. Choose a product, service, or idea which could be expressed by means of a poster.
   b. Make several thumb nail sketches of layouts for your poster.
   c. Select the layout which seems to have the best design possibilities, and select the tools and materials which you wish to use for the poster.
   d. Now construct the poster.
   e. Evaluate the poster according to the principles of design.

10

THE END AND THE BEGINNING

The last chapter of the book is obviously "The End," but how is "The Beginning" related to this? This textbook was planned to help students, as consumers and producers, to develop an awareness and understanding of good design. Understanding cannot take place until there is first an awareness. The experiments at the end of the chapters dealing with elements of design were planned with two goals in mind. The combination of these two should help you to begin developing an understanding of design. The first part of the experiments was planned to help you see, discover, and develop an awareness. The second portion was planned to help you create "your own designs." The entire text has stressed "your own" designs; however, Alexander Girard says, "Designs that are fresh, interesting and different are not achieved if to be fresh, interesting and different is the prime objective." He further states "Good design derives from the wish to do just that."

We must stress that the mechanical act of seeing in itself is not awareness. Awareness results in conscious perceiving. This perceiving not only includes seeing and feeling but also registering the response from your total being.

With the dawning of your awareness, understanding can develop. This understanding involves making critical judgements. In relationship of understanding to design you need to develop a sensitivity to design ele-

Fig. 10-1. A student plans her design for a mosaic table top. (Photograph courtesy of Texas Technological College.)

(lower left)
Fig. 10-2. A student is shown weaving with strips of bamboo over colorful warp yarns to make a wall panel. (Photograph courtesy of Texas Technological College.)

(lower right)
Fig. 10-3. Scraps of metal are no longer "scrap" when welded together in a piece of metal sculpture like "The Squawker." (Sculpture by Bill Lockhart. Photograph courtesy of Texas Technological College.)

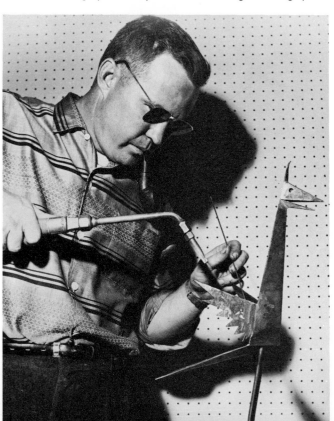

Fig. 10-4. Printed warp by means of the silk-screen process adds interest to a handwoven fabric. Weaving by Elva Powell. (Photograph courtesy of Texas Technological College.)

Fig. 10-5. A student experiments with the silk-screen printing process. (Photograph courtesy of Texas Technological College.)

Fig. 10-6. Students in the boys' dormitory discuss the enamel-on-copper wallpiece which hangs in their lounge. Design for wallpiece by Bill Lockhart. (Photograph courtesy of Texas Technological College.)

Fig. 10-7. Zodiac signs in poplar on walnut and mahogony backgrounds with bright spots of color added in bits of enamel-on-copper. Design by Ethel Jane Beitler. (Photograph courtesy of Design Today, Inc.)

Fig. 10-8. A dramatic color combination of blue-green, blue, and blue-violet for a nonobjective pattern in a hooked rug. (Original student design by Mickey Story.)

ments. Your evaluation comes from your application of the guideposts or principles of design to the organization of the elements.

Whether your interest in design will be from the consumer's or producer's point of view, this is the beginning. Girard says, "The hope for good design lies in those designers who believe in what they do and who will only do what they believe. . . ." We further believe that the same is true for the consumer. Are our selections made by what the Jones have, or what is popular, or do we have the nerve to select what is the best design for us? The authors feel that with increased understanding of design you not only create a more functional environment but you can also develop a more satisfying environment for your spirit.

When asked what went into a good design, a designer said, "It takes the eye, the hand, the brain, and the heart!" Does it not follow that understanding of good design will also affect these same separate parts in an integrated pattern?

One of the last things that the late Walter Dorwin Teague wrote seems to sum up so well his design philosophy.

> Design is like a river that flows slowly. It makes no abrupt changes of direction but over the years its character gradually varies. It carries on its current many beautiful things out of the past which we still treasure even though we have no desire to copy them today. We should hope that the things we do now will have similar values for the future.

Fig. 10-9. Steel, wire, and washers welded together to give a flexible movement in space. (Designer, Bill Lockhart. Owner, Martye Poindexter.)

GLOSSARY

TERMS PERTAINING TO DESIGN

Abstract. Portraying a basic shape without imitating appearances. The shapes may be simplified, exaggerated, or rearranged.

Applied Art. A phrase often used to describe those arts which are made by craftsmen.

Asymmetric. Not symmetrical. Usually much more free than formal balance. Also referred to as occult, or informal.

Balance. A principle of design which presents an impression of equal distribution of weight in a design.

Baroque. A type of late Renaissance art which was a reaction from standardized classic forms in the direction of greater freedom. Baroque art is often characterized by strong contrasts and elaborately twisted and curved forms.

Biomorphic. Forms related to life or living organisms, such as a bean or a pear.

Bisymmetrical Balance. Identical elements or powers of attraction placed equally from the center of a design.

Bizarre. Strikingly out of the ordinary or out of keeping, especially as to fashion, design, color, and the like.

Calligraphy. Beauty of lines, varying in widths, curve, rhythm, etc.

Cartoon. A comic drawing. It may be satirical in nature. It may also be an artist's drawing to serve as a model for a fresco, mosaic, tapestry, etc.

Character. In art, character refers to individuality, creativeness, or a satisfying expression of imagination.

191

Classic. Belonging to the culture and art of the ancient Greeks and Romans.

Collage. An organization of elements in a semiflat abstract manner. It is mainly an experiment in combination of textures.

Composition. The product of an arrangement of related parts; design, organization.

Congruity. Harmony of the various parts of elements of design with the whole.

Continuity. An orderly sequence of the parts of a design from one to the other and to the whole.

Contour. The line bounding a shape or form; outline.

Decorative Design. The design which is added to the surface of a structural design for the purpose of enriching it.

Design. An organization of the elements of design with two aims, order and beauty.

Diagonal. Oblique—expressing motion or a bracing effect against an opposite force.

Dimension. In art in general: any measurable extent, as breadth, length, or thickness. In color: a property or characteristic, such as hue, value, or intensity.

Distortion. A change from normal proportions. A twisting or writhing motion or misshapen condition.

Dominance. Superiority in size, placement, or general character.

Dynamic. Giving an effect of movement, energy, force.

Eclectic. Selecting and combining from various doctrines, systems, or styles that which is thought best. Most of our present-day houses which were built twenty-five or more years ago are eclectic; borrowing from such historic examples as the Colonial, French Provincial, or Tudor.

Elements of Design. Tools and materials to use in making a design. The elements of design are: line, shape, space, color, and texture.

Elevation. A drawing showing no perspective, but is a flat view, of the front, side, or rear of an object.

Emphasis. A principle of design which leads the eye first to the most important part of a design and to all other parts in the order of their importance.

Esthetic. Pertaining to beauty, taste, or the fine arts; artistic. Appreciating or loving the beautiful.

Exotic. Belonging to another part of the world; foreign; strange.

Expressionism. Art in which the emphasis is on inner emotions, sensations, or ideas rather than actual appearances.

Fashion. The prevailing mode; manner of doing a thing.

Form. In art, a three-dimensional object.

Formal. Made or done in accordance with regular or established forms and methods, or with proper dignity and impressiveness; orderly.

Formal Balance. Organization of identical or similar elements or powers of attraction placed equal distances from the center so there is equal distribution of weight on both sides.

Free-Form. Shapes or forms which do not follow any set of rules; biomorphic.

Geometric. Characterized by regular lines, curves, and angles, as in geometry.

Good Taste. Application of the principles of design to the problems in life where utility and beauty are considerations.

Graphic Processes. Those processes for printing or reproduction of drawings, photographs, etc.

Grotesque. An unnatural but decorative combination of human and animal forms interwoven with plant forms; also applied to art forms which are awkward or incongruous.

Harmony. The resulting attribute when the principles of design present an impression of unity with sufficient variety to add interest.

Horizontal. Parallel to the horizon; suggests or conveys a feeling of repose.

Impressionism. A movement in art, particularly painting, in which the aim was to preserve the vividness and force of the first impression nature makes on the painter's vision and to convey the sensation of movement and light. Impressionism is often associated with artists such as Seurat, Manet, Monet, who used broken color in small dots or brush strokes which blended together in the eye of the observer.

Informal Balance. Organization of unlike elements or powers of attraction placed unequal distances from the center of a design so there is equal distribution of weight on both sides. Sometimes referred to as occult or asymmetrical balance.

Isometric Drawing. A drawing in which no attempt has been made to show perspective, but lines have been made parallel and at right angles to each other.

Layout. A term used in printing and in commercial art referring to the arrangement of pictures and words on the page.

Lettering. The process of making letters by hand with pencil, lettering pen, etc.

Linear. Pertaining to or composed of lines. Very narrow and long.

Mechanical Spacing. Spacing which is measured with a ruler or other mechanical means.

Medium. The material used to produce an art object. Also the liquid which is used to mix pigments to make them suitable for painting. Also the middle value of gray on the standard value scale.

Mobile. A three-dimensional abstraction which usually hangs from the ceiling and has moving parts which rotate as the currents of air strike them.

Montage. A picture or page arrangement made by grouping or superimposing several pictures so as to blend into one another, or so as to show figures upon a desired background; a composite picture; also a process of composing a picture.

Mosaic. A type of inlaid decoration, composed of small pieces of stone or glass, generally used for the decoration of walls and floors, but recently used for table tops.

Motif. A distinct principal idea or element of design.

Mural. A painting or decoration on a wall.

Nonobjective. Referring to painting and sculpture which are expressions in pure form and design showing no resemblance to natural objects.

Objective. A goal; that toward which effort is directed; an aim; an end.

Opposition. Diametrical differences in position—variation in direction of lines.

Optical Illusion. An unreal image seemingly presented to the senses; any misleading appearance; false perception.

Optical Spacing. Spacing which is measured by the eye as a gauge.

Organic. Having the character of living forms. Organic art, such as the houses of Frank Lloyd Wright, shows the vitality and unity found in animals and plants.

Organization. The systematic relation of parts to each other and to the whole; design.

Pattern. Anything shaped or formed to serve as a model or guide in forming something else. Any decorative design, usually in a planned repeat.

Perspective. The art of representing, by a drawing made on a flat surface, solid objects or surfaces conceived of as not lying on that surface; representing objects as they appear to the eye. The art of conveying the impression of distance and depth.

Picturesque. Having a striking or irregular beauty, quaintness, or charm.

Pigment. Any coloring material, but usually dry earth mineral, or vegetable compound, which is mixed with a liquid to produce paint.

Plane. Any flat or uncurved surface.

Precept. A working rule or law.

Plastic Elements. Line, shape, form, space, color, and texture; the elements of which all products of the plastic and graphic arts are composed.

Principles of Design. Guideposts to use in evaluating the organization of the elements of design. The principles of design are: balance, proportion, emphasis, and rhythm.

Printing. The act of reproducing a design upon a surface by means of any graphic process.

Proportion. A principle of design which deals with the relationship between each part of a design in relation to each other and to the whole design.

Radiation. Lines or parts of a design growing out of, or extending from, a line or a point.

Realism. The representation of things as they are in life without idealizing them.

Repeat. A term used to denote one complete unit of a repeated design.

Renaissance. The great revival in art and learning in Europe beginning in the fifteenth century in Italy. The Renaissance began in Italy and quickly spread to the other countries of Europe. Artistically, it involved the rejection of the Gothic style and the revival of the classical Roman style and ideas.

Representational. Characterized by a likeness to or depicting persons and scenes as they exist, without any attempt at idealization.

Rhythm. A principle of design which provides an easily connected path over which the eye may travel.

Rococco. A type of Renaissance ornament developed during the seventeenth and eighteenth centures in which rocks and rocklike forms were combined with fantastic scrolls, shells, etc., to present a lavish but often confused display of decoration.

Scale. The size of the parts in relation to the whole object or a representation of an object to the object itself.

Sculpture. Figures or arrangements of forms carved, cut, hewn, cast, or modeled in wood, stone, clay, or metal.

Shape. A two-dimensional flat object.

Simulate. To assume or have the mere appearance or form of, without the reality; imitate.

Stabile. A three-dimensional abstraction which has no moving parts like a mobile.

Static. At rest or in complete equilibrium; suggesting no movement; opposite to dynamic.

Structural Design. The design made by the size, shape, color, and texture of an object, whether it be the actual object or a representation of it on paper.

Still Life. A painting of objects, such as fruits, flowers, vases, etc., as distinguished from those of landscapes or people.

Subordination. To hold of less importance; minor.

Surrealism. A type of painting in which the artist paints the images from the subconscious self rather than what he sees about him. Surrealism is an attempt to go beyond actual observation, and paintings are likely to be full of symbolism.

Symbolic. Representation by symbols rather than by imitation.

Symmetry. A balancing of parts in which those on one side of the center are the exact reverse of those on the other. Formal balance.

Tactual. Pertaining to the sense of touch.

Technique. Method or way of doing something, such as the way to hold a brush or the amount of pressure to place upon it to make particular types of strokes.

Tempera. Opaque water color, or an opaque paint in which the pigment is mixed with an albuminous substance, frequently white of egg rather than oil or water.

Tension. Any strained relations. Tensions in art are the representations of the pulling forces between parts of the composition.

Texture. Surface characteristics.

Tonal. The general color scheme or collective tones of a picture or composition.

Traditional. Handed down from one generation to another; still having usefulness.

Transition. Leading the eye easily from one part of a design to another. Growing out of it.

Unity. Similarity. Of equal importance. Oneness.

Vertical. Standing erect—suggest upward force.

Void. Empty; free; producing no effect.

TERMS PERTAINING TO COLOR

Classes of Color

Primary, secondary or binary, intermediate, normal, standard, or popular.

Acid Colors. Cool colors, such as cyan-blue, ultramarine, magenta, which we associate with the color of acids.

Advancing Colors. The warm colors, or those of bright intensity that seem to advance.

Cool Colors. Cool colors are those which have blue in their mixture, as green, blue-green. Violet is on the borderline between warm and cool.

Earth Colors. Colors, such as ombre, yellow ochre, mustard, terra cotta, which are found in the earth's strata.

Intermediate Hues. A mixture of one primary and one secondary. Yellow-green, blue-green, blue-violet, red-violet, red-orange, and yellow-orange are the six intermediate hues.

Normal Hue. The pure color; the brightest intensity that it is possible for a color to be.

Popular Hue. A name given to a special value or intensity of a color by a manufacturer for the purpose of "popularizing" it for a particular product, season, etc.

Primary Hues. The basic colors from which are derived all the other colors. Red, blue, and yellow are the three primary hues.

Receding Colors. The cool colors or the ones which are grayed in intensity seem to recede.

Secondary or Binary Hues. A mixture of two primary hues. Green, orange, and violet are the three secondary hues.

Standard Hue. The six major hues on the color wheel: red, yellow, blue, green, orange, and violet.

Warm Colors. Warm colors are those which have red in their mixture, as red-orange, orange. Yellow is sometimes considered a warm hue because of its association with sunshine.

Color Harmony

Colors used together for a particular purpose and giving the impression that they belong together.

Color Theory

An arrangement of colors for the purpose of study.

Chemist's Color Theory. Studies color from the chemical properties of pigments as used for dyes and paints.

Munsell Color Theory. Another color system. Five primary hues (red, blue, yellow, green, and purple); and five secondary hues (yellow-red, green-yellow, blue-green, blue-purple, and red-purple).

Psychologist's Color Theory. Studies color from the way it affects the mind and emotions.

Physicist's Color Theory. Studies wavelengths and intensities. Light theory.

Physiologist's Color Theory. Studies color from the way in which it is received by the eye. Fatigue experiments.

Prang Color Theory. One of the color systems. Three primary hues (red, blue, and yellow); three secondary hues (green, orange, and violet); and six intermediate hues (yellow-green, yellow-orange, blue-green, blue-violet, red-violet, and red-orange).

Color Wheel

The arrangement of colors in their correct order in relation to their mixtures. The complements are opposite to each other, the line connecting them going through the center of the circle.

Contrasting Hues

Hues which have no color in common, such as blue and orange.

Contrasting Intensities

Some bright and some dull intensities used together.

Contrasting Values

Values which are not near each other on the value scale.

Dimension or Property

The three characteristics or ways in which colors differ: hue, value, and intensity.

Hue. The name of the color, such as red, green, blue-green.

Intensity. The brightness or dullness of colors.

Value. The lightness or darkness of colors.

Gradation of Hue

Closely related hues which show a gradual change from one hue into another; such as yellow, yellow-green, green, blue-green.

Gradation of Intensity

Closely related intensities which show a gradual change from one intensity to another; as bright, slightly grayed, moderately grayed, dull.

Gradation of Value

Closely related values which show a gradual change from one value into another; such as high-light, light, low-light, medium.

High Intensities

Hues which are bright in intensity; normal, pure pigment.

High Value

A value above medium on the value scale.

Low Intensities

Hues which are dull in intensity; have been grayed considerably.

Low Value

A value below medium on the value scale.

Lower the Intensity

To make duller; add the complement or a neutral.

Lower the Value

To make darker in value; add black or more pigment.

Major Contrast

Large interval, strong contrast.

Mechanical Color Combination

Colors selected from a mechanical arrangement on the color wheel, not necessarily harmonious with each other until the values, intensities, and amounts are taken into consideration for the purpose for which the colors will be used.

Analogous. Neighboring or adjacent hues, related, having a color in common.

Complement. The color opposite another on the color wheel, the line connecting the two going through the center of the circle, as red and green.

Double-Complement. Combinations of two hues with their corresponding complements, such as yellow-orange and yellow-green with red-violet and blue-violet.

Monochromatic. The use of one hue in a variety of values.

Split-Complement. Combinations of a hue with the hues on either side of its complement, such as yellow with red-violet and blue-violet.

Triad. Use of three hues which are equally distant on the color wheel, such as red, yellow, and blue.

Minor Contrast

Small interval, closely related, similar.

Miscellaneous Color Terms

Color Path. A series of colors showing a gradation in one or more dimensions.

Dissonance. A satisfactory use of reverse order of values; like a minor key in music.

High Key Colors. Those colors which are normally light in value, or those which have been raised in value to those above medium on the value scale.

Law of Areas. Large areas should be quiet in effect with small areas showing strong contrast of hue, value, or intensity.

Low Key Colors. Those colors which are normally dark in value, or those which have been lowered in value to those below medium on the value scale.

GLOSSARY

Natural Order of Values. Hues selected in the same order of values as the normal equivalents are found on the standard value scale. For instance, normal green is the equivalent of low-light, whereas normal blue-green is the equivalent of medium. Whenever these two hues are used together and the green is a lighter form than the blue-green, they are said to be in the natural order of values.

Neutral. Gray, black, or white.

Neutralize. To gray, or dull, or lower the intensity of a color by the addition of the complement or a neutral.

Pastel. A light value in a grayed intensity.

Reverse Order of Values. Contrary to the order of values of hues as the pure pigments are shown on the standard value scale. For instance, normal green is the equivalent of low-light, whereas normal blue-green is the equivalent of medium. When blue-green is made the equivalent of high-light and the green is made the equivalent of high-dark, they are in reverse order of values.

Saturation. Full strength of pure pigment.

Shade. A value of a color darker than the normal.

Spectrum. The band of successive colors which appear when a ray of sunlight is passed through a prism, breaking up the light into a sequence of strong colors.

Tint. A value of a color lighter than the normal.

Tone. The prevailing effect of a color brought about by blending.

Normal Value Scale

The steps on the standard value scale from white to black, with the normal hues placed in relation to their equivalent values.

Raise the Intensity

To make brighter; add more pure pigment.

Raise the Value

To make lighter in value; add black or more pigment.

Related Hues

Several hues which have a hue in common, such as yellow, yellow-green, and green all have yellow in common.

Related Intensities

Intensities which are similar—all bright or all grayed.

Related Values

Values which are close to each other on the value scale.

Standard Value Scale

The steps of dark and light between white, seven values of gray, and black.

Value Key

A system or series of values based on their relation to a dominant value.

High Major Key. If there is an interval of five or more steps between the darkest and lightest values, strong contrast results, and it may be called a high major key if there is a larger area of light value than dark.

High Minor Key. If the darkest and lighest values in the design are no more than three steps apart, it may be called a high minor key if they are all values above medium on the value scale.

Intermediate Major Key. Strong contrast of values with a larger area of medium value (a value from the middle part of the value scale).

Intermediate Minor Key. Closely related values all low-light, medium, or high-dark.

Low Major Key. Strong contrast of values with a larger area of dark value than light.

Low Minor Key. Closely related values all below medium value.

INDEX

203